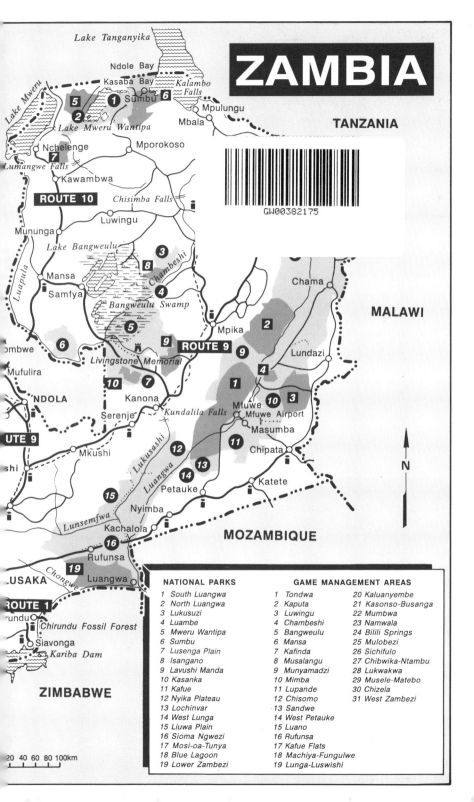

ZAMBIA

Lake Tanganyika

Ndole Bay
Kasaba Bay
Sumbu
Kalambo Falls
Mpulungu
Mbala

TANZANIA

Lake Mweru
Lake Mweru Wantipa

Nchelenge
Mporokoso
Lumangwe Falls
Kawambwa

ROUTE 10
Chisimba Falls

GW00382175

Luwingu

Munungu
Lake Bangweulu
Chambeshi

Mansa
Samfya

Chama

MALAWI

Bangweulu Swamp
Mpika

ombwe
Livingstone Memorial
ROUTE 9
Lundazi

Mufulira
NDOLA
Kanona
Kundalila Falls
Mfuwe
Mfuwe Airport
Masumba

shi
Serenje
UTE 9
Mkushi
Lukusashi
Chipata
Katete

Lukusashi
Luangwa
Petauke
Nyimba
Lunsemfwa
Kachalola

MOZAMBIQUE

N

Rufunsa
USAKA
Chongwe
Luangwa

ROUTE 1
undu
Chirundu Fossil Forest
Siavonga
Kariba Dam

ZIMBABWE

20 40 60 80 100km

NATIONAL PARKS	GAME MANAGEMENT AREAS	
1 South Luangwa	1 Tondwa	20 Kaluanyembe
2 North Luangwa	2 Kaputa	21 Kasonso-Busanga
3 Lukusuzi	3 Luwingu	22 Mumbwa
4 Luambe	4 Chambeshi	23 Namwala
5 Mweru Wantipa	5 Bangweulu	24 Bilili Springs
6 Sumbu	6 Mansa	25 Mulobezi
7 Lusenga Plain	7 Kafinda	26 Sichifulo
8 Isangano	8 Musalangu	27 Chibwika-Ntambu
9 Lavushi Manda	9 Munyamadzi	28 Lukwakwa
10 Kasanka	10 Mimba	29 Musele-Matebo
11 Kafue	11 Lupande	30 Chizela
12 Nyika Plateau	12 Chisomo	31 West Zambezi
13 Lochinvar	13 Sandwe	
14 West Lunga	14 West Petauke	
15 Liuwa Plain	15 Luano	
16 Sioma Ngwezi	16 Rufunsa	
17 Mosi-oa-Tunya	17 Kafue Flats	
18 Blue Lagoon	18 Machiya-Fungulwe	
19 Lower Zambezi	19 Lunga-Luswishi	

VISITORS' GUIDE TO ZAMBIA

VISITORS' GUIDE TO ZAMBIA

HOW TO GET THERE · WHAT TO SEE · WHERE TO STAY

Nicholas Plewman
Brendan Dooley

SOUTHERN
BOOK PUBLISHERS

ISBN 1 86812 532 7

First edition, first impression 1995
First edition, second impression 1996

Published by
Southern Book Publishers (Pty) Ltd
PO Box 3103, Halfway House 1685

While the authors and publisher have endeavoured
to verify all facts, they will not be held responsible
for any inconvenience that may result from
possible inaccuracies in this book.

Cover photograph by N Plewman
Cover design by Insight Graphics
Maps by Ingrid Booysen
Set in 10/11.5 pt Palatino
by Kohler Carton & Print, Pinetown
Printed and bound by Kohler Carton & Print, Pinetown

ACKNOWLEDGEMENTS

It would not have been possible to research and write this book without the assistance of a great number of people in many and varied ways and to them the authors owe a debt of gratitude. We would like to express heartfelt thanks to the following: The Director of the Zambia National Tourist Board, Mr George Lewis and his staff in Lusaka and Donald Pelekamoyo of ZNTB, Johannesburg, Moira Smith and Zambia Airways, the Managing Director of BP Zambia, Mr Peter Knoedel for his generous sponsorship of a large part of our fuel requirements, the Director of The National Heritage Conservation Commission, Mr Nicholas Katanekwa, for historical advice, the Chairman of the Hotel and Catering Association, Mr Gaudenzio Rossi, for help with accommodation, all the lodge and hotel owners throughout the country who opened their establishments to us and all the organisations who provided information to us. To the numerous Samaritans who helped keep "the antichrist", our Land Rover, on the road against all odds and to all those who took us in along the way, especially the missionaries at Chavuma, Likulu, Kalabo, Sioma and Serenje, Sheila Siddle at Chimfunshi and Pete and Lynn Fisher at Hillwood Farm – thank you all. In addition, very special thanks to David and Mark Harvey, Ron and Megan Landless, and David and Joan Littleford for their tireless hospitality and encouragement.

Lastly, with love and thanks we dedicate this book to the best and most companionable of fellow travellers, Louise and Kathy, without whom we would never have crossed the Zambezi.

CONTENTS

INTRODUCTION

The name Zambia will conjure up widely different pictures to different people. Such is the legacy of recent history both in the country and in southern Africa as a whole that those who have never been there can even be forgiven for not knowing quite where it is and imagining perhaps a vaguely defined primordial swamp territory wallowing in a tropical stew of post-colonial anarchy.

It is the purpose of this book to dispel that notion and to reveal instead a country with an ancient and fascinating history that is now a stable democracy with a hard-pressed but stalwart economy and the wonderful resources of warm-hearted people, huge tracts of pristine environment and an established tourist infrastructure.

Zambia has been ill served by travel literature to date. Prior to 1991 it probably deserved this and numerous horror stories emerged of travellers being so harassed at every turn by both officials and criminals that it was difficult to tell the difference between them. After many months of travel through the very furthest reaches of Zambia, the authors must say at the outset that nothing could be less true about the country that we found. On the contrary, the people as a whole are overwhelmingly friendly. Officials are usually courteous and helpful. There is crime in the major urban centres, but no more so and perhaps much less so than in most big cities in the world. Today Zambia is probably one of the safest countries in Africa to travel in.

Although parts of the infrastructure are in disrepair it remains quite serviceable and enterprising tourists will find few serious impediments to travel in the country. Without doubt the major attractions in Zambia are the game reserves and wilderness areas and the rivers and lakes with which they are associated. Distances are great and roads slow but whether it be amongst elephants on the sandy shore of Lake Tanganyika, countless thousands of antelope on the Kafue Flats, or venerable cultures like the Lozi of Barotseland, visitors to Zambia are assured of experiences that simply cannot be enjoyed in any other country on the subcontinent.

HOW TO USE THIS GUIDE

Chapter 1 introduces Zambia and explains how it came to be the country that it is. Chapters 2, 3 and 4 outline the options for getting to and around the country and preparations you should make beforehand. Then read chapter 5, which broadly outlines the activities available to visitors, special considerations in Zambia affecting those activities and where best to pursue them.

Chapters 6 to 11 tell where to go and how to get there in more detail. Zambia is divided into eight administrative provinces (see section on geography, chapter 1). However, other than for certain bureaucratic functions this division is of little consequence to the visitor. For the purpose of describing routes and destinations in the country, the map of Zambia can be divided into six regions of interest and they are described by chapter as follows:

Chapter 6: The Central Region; including Central and Lusaka provinces, west to the Kafue National Park as far north as Kapiri Mposhi and south to Chirundu and the Lower Zambezi National Park.

Chapter 7: The Southern Region; between the lower Zambezi River and the Kafue River Flats and between Victoria Falls and the Kariba Dam.

Chapter 8: The Western Region; including both sides of the upper Zambezi between its source right up in the north-west corner of the country and the Victoria Falls.

Chapter 9: The Copperbelt; including all the mining towns north of Kapiri Mposhi.

Chapter 10: The Northern Region; includes the Zaïre watershed between the Great North Road, Zaïre and the lakes.

Chapter 11: The Eastern Region; the Luangwa Valley between the Great North Road watershed and the Malawi border.

Routes 1 to 11 shown on the endpaper maps are described at the end of each regional chapter. In addition to directions and distances, details that may make the journey interesting or diverting are included in these routes.

Most places to stay are mentioned in the regional chapters, but there is a detailed directory of addresses and telephone numbers in chapter 12.

Chapter 13 gives further directories as well as useful tips and information.

Distances given in the routes are only approximate. Note that distance measurement tends to vary from vehicle to vehicle. Zambia's tourist industry is expanding rapidly and tourist operations are being established all the time. Consult travel agents for further information.

1 THE FACTORS THAT SHAPE ZAMBIA

HISTORY

Pre-Colonial history

Human history in south-central Africa goes back millions of years. Zambia has scores of archaeological sites from the Victoria Falls on the Zambezi all the way up to the shores of Lake Tanganyika that provide evidence of human occupation from the earliest Stone Age through the Iron Age to within the recollection of oral tradition and contemporary history. A great number of such sites have been documented and preserved by the National Heritage Conservation Commission of Zambia, although hitherto most have been neglected as a source of tourist interest.

Tools found in the Zambezi Valley below Victoria Falls compare with those from East Africa dated up to 2,5 million years ago. There is evidence at the same sites of hominid advancement and a gradual improvement in tool-making until 70 000 years ago. At Kalambo Falls above Lake Tanganyika there is evidence of the earliest fire-making from this time and at the Broken Hill mine, now Kabwe, perhaps Zambia's most famous archaeological discovery was made – *Homo rhodesiensis*, a skull that became known as Broken Hill Man and dates from this period. Perhaps under the influence of environmental change, about 50 000 years ago these Early Stone Age hominids began to spread out from the river valleys and occupy caves on the open plateau.

The steady evolution of the species can be traced in Zambia by the refinements of tool-making until the appearance of modern man – evidenced in another discovery at Broken Hill of a jawbone that more closely resembles our own than that of the previously discovered skull.

The Stone Age progressed through further environmental changes and an increase in population until most of the region was occupied. While tradition holds that these Stone Age dwellers in caves and rock shelters were Khoisan people or Bushmen, there is some evidence to suggest that they were rather of Negroid stock. Bushmen Stone Age cultures did survive until comparatively recently, particularly in southwestern Zambia.

Excavations near Sesheke on the upper Zambezi have revealed pottery shards of an Iron Age culture as early as 310 BC; no longer just hunter-gatherers, the people practised agriculture, kept stock and settled in villages of wattle and daub houses. Iron-working appears to coincide with the immigration of large numbers of Bantu language speaking people.

This Bantu colonisation seems to have occurred in three waves and from three directions. The first movement came up the Zambezi Valley from the east, moving as far as Sesheke three centuries before Christ. In the sixth century AD another wave migrated down the Zambezi from the north. Both these migrations brought cattle with them. Then in the 9th century a large group moved down from the Zaïre Basin. These people did not own cattle but began to assimilate the peoples who had preceded them, and by the 11th century they were in the majority. Smelting of both iron and copper were well under way and with the development of wealth and power nation-states emerged in the kingdoms of the Kazembe, Lunda, Lozi and Chewa.

Colonial history

A fairly substantial trade, carried out mainly by the Arabs, existed between central Africa and lands across the Indian Ocean before the coming of the Europeans. Then in the 15th century the Portuguese, lured by rumours of fabulous wealth in the kingdom of Mwene Mutapa south of the Zambezi, began exploring the valley and establishing bases on the Mozambique coast. They made little effort at real colonisation, spending their resources on ill-conceived expeditions of plunder, but over the succeeding centuries trader-adventurers began penetrating the interior.

In 1793 a Goanese, Goncalo Pereira, became the first European to substantially explore what is today Zambia, venturing as far as the kingdom of Kazembe, south of Lake Mweru. At approximately the same time Portuguese traders from Angola made journeys as far as the headwaters of the Zambezi and in 1795 reached the Barotse floodplains.

At the beginning of the 19th century events took place in southern Africa that would dramatically affect the future of the territory.

Under the dual pressure of slaving by Portuguese and Arabs on the east coast and European settler advance from the Cape, an extraordinary and terrible chain of events was set in motion by the rise of the Zulu nation and their systematic conquering and destruction of tribes around them. The only escape was flight and the plunder of new lands, which gave rise to a domino sequence that spread right up into central Africa and was known as the "*Difaqane*".

Cutting a swathe of destruction as they went, the Ngoni people moved up in the east through Zimbabwe to eventually settle in Zambia, Malawi and Tanzania. The Kololo, who were Basotho people, fled the terror westwards right across the Kalahari Desert as far as the Zambezi.

After conquering the Batonga, the Kololo settled in what is today southern Zambia. Fearful of attack by the Matabele, who had fought their way into Zimbabwe under a dissident Zulu general, Mzilikazi, the Kololo leader Sebitoane took advantage of the recent death of the Lozi king to annex Barotseland as well. David Livingstone was present when Sebitoane died in 1851, on the threshold of a new era in central Africa.

When Livingstone returned in 1855 Sekeletu, Sebitoane's son, showed him the falls, which he named the Victoria Falls on 16 November 1855. Thereafter the passage of European pioneers increased. Two of the most prominent were George Westbeech, an ivory hunter and trader, and Francois Coillard, a missionary, both of whom had a profound effect on future developments in the region. Livingstone, of course went on to explore what is now north-eastern Zambia and the lake region, bringing to the world's attention the enormous Arab-controlled slave trade that had blossomed there before he eventually died on the eastern side of Lake Bangeweulu.

The exploits of Livingstone and other missionaries and traders put the region north of the Zambezi on the map. Cecil Rhodes's British South Africa Company expressed interest in the territory's potential mineral wealth, while the British Crown was interested in stamping out the slave trade as well as securing land ahead of its European rivals. By the 1880s the scramble for Africa was on. Anxious to prevent the Portuguese from pursuing their plans of joining Angola with Mozambique, Rhodes sent one Frank Lochner to Lealui, the Barotseland capital. Deceitfully proclaiming himself an emissary of the British queen, Lochner persuaded the king, Lewanika, to sign over all mineral rights to the British South Africa Company.

At the same time British officials from British Central Africa (Malawi) made administrative forays into what is today northern Zambia, to seek alliances with local chiefs and stamp out the ongoing Arab slave trade, gradually bringing the region under British control. It became known as North-eastern Rhodesia and had its capital at Fort Jameson, today called Chipata. Barotseland and the west was incorporated into Northwestern Rhodesia with a capital at Kalomo before it was moved to Livingstone in 1907. Although formally part of the British empire, both territories were controlled under Royal Charter by the British South Africa Company. In 1911 the territories were joined to become simply Northern Rhodesia with Livingstone remaining the capital. Between 1911 and 1914 an Anglo-Belgian boundary commission established the position of the territory's northern border. Having made little effort to settle and develop the region, the British South Africa Company handed over Northern Rhodesia to the British Government in 1924.

With the beginning of large-scale copper mining in the north and gradual settlement of the rest of the country, a more centralised administrative centre was required and in 1930 the capital was moved to the hitherto rather undeveloped railway town of Lusaka. In 1953 agitation by settler communities led to the amalgamation of Northern Rhodesia with Southern Rhodesia and Nyasaland to form the Central African Federation. Ill-conceived, the Federation could not withstand the growing tide of African nationalism and the desire for majority rule and self-government in each territory. Short lived as the Federation was, it had a staggering affect on Zambia. The book *Africa on a Shoestring* (Lonely Planet 1989) quotes some devastating statistics. During Federation some US $200 million created in Northern Rhodesia was spent in Southern Rhodesia. By the time the colonial era drew to a close the British South Africa Company had extracted about $160 million in mining "royalties". The British Treasury had collected $80 million in taxes but spent only $10 million on the territory. Subsequent abuses notwithstanding, that imbalance between exploitation and investment is written bold across every mile of Zambian infrastructure.

The Federation was dissolved in 1963 and on 24 October 1964 Northern Rhodesia became the independent Republic of Zambia with Dr Kenneth David Kaunda as president. Although the country was nominally a democracy, in 1972 the constitution was amended to make it a one-party state with Kaunda's party, the United Independence Party (UNIP) the only party. Obsessed with an African socialist philosophy that he called "Humanism", Kenneth Kaunda or KK as he became known, nationalised almost every sector of the economy. In doing so he bound the country's fortunes even more tightly to the copper mines and when the bottom fell out of the copper market, Zambia plunged with it (see section on Economy). At the same time KK's African socialist ideals led him to support a string of liberation armies fighting in neighbouring countries. In return the Rhodesians and South Africans laid waste to road and rail infrastructure in a long campaign of sabotage and intimidation. Subsequent food and commodity shortages provoked widespread instability and produced the violent paranoia about national security that made travel in the country so unpleasant. To this day it is extraordinary how little Zambians know about their country as a whole. Popular dissatisfaction grew until in 1990 Kaunda capitulated and agreed to a multi-party election under the misconception that he would be returned to power. Instead the winners of the first democratic election in nearly 30 years were the liberal capitalist Movement for Multiparty Democracy, the MMD, and they currently rule with President Frederick Chiluba as leader.

GEOGRAPHY

Size:	750 000 square kilometres
Altitude:	1 300 m above sea level, average
Climate:	Subtropical
Population:	About 8 million

Zambia, landlocked in south-central Africa, is a vast, kidney-shaped plateau most of which drains gently southward to the great Zambezi River. Its shape may seem absurd but its boundaries conform to geographical features such as watersheds and rivers. Although well within the tropics, between 10 and 18 degrees south of the Equator, it is a temperate land since it has a relatively high altitude. It is well watered with big rivers, swamps and lakes. It is generally flat and well wooded. Being such a large country it is bounded by no fewer than eight other countries, whose borders are divided along major rivers and watersheds. Zambia borders on Zaïre, Tanzania, Malawi, Mozambique, Zimbabwe, Botswana, Namibia and Angola.

The country is divided into eight provinces, the divisions corresponding roughly with the changing topography. The Zambezi River rises from its forested upland watershed in North-western Province, just kilometres away from the Zaïre border where the land tips northward and begins emptying its rivers into the Zaïre Basin. Thence it flows into Angola and out again, southward into Western Province and Barotseland, a flat region of vast grass plains, floodplain and dry woodland. Southern Province extends from the flat lands around the hook of the

Kafue River, southwards to where the Zambezi divides Zambia from Namibia, Botswana and Zimbabwe and falls over the Victoria Falls into the valleys of the Batoka Gorge and Kariba.

Between the tributaries of the Kafue and Luangwa rivers lies hilly Lusaka Province. Central Province, between Lusaka and Kapiri Mposhi where the Great North Road turns east, is the developed farming heartland of the country. North of Lusaka lies rich farmland and north of that again, Copperbelt Province with its towns and cities close strung along the seams of ore from which it gets its name. Here a narrow strip of Zaïre known as the Congo pedicle almost cuts Zambia in two.

The two halves are connected by the Great North Road which runs into Northern Province along an undulating escarpment. To one side of the road lies the basin of the Bangeweulu Swamp, from where the Luapula River ultimately runs into the Zaïre River. On the other side the plateau collapses down the Muchinga Escarpment into the Luangwa Valley which runs eventually into the Zambezi on the border with Mozambique. Northern Province straddles the watershed right up to Lake Tanganyika. To its west lies Luapula Province, mostly flat country falling westwards to the Zaïre border along the Luapula River and Lake Mweru. On the other side of the Luangwa lies Eastern Province, rising up to the Nyika Plateau and the highest point in the land at 2 148 m on the border with Malawi.

POPULATION

Zambia's eight million people are mostly Africans of Bantu origin (see section on History) belonging to a large number of tribes speaking 73 different dialects, although the *lingua franca* is English (see Language, chapter 2). From its colonial history Zambia has inherited a thriving expatriate community, largely British in origin, and Asians who settled under the British and now live and work in the major business centres. Recently other nationalities have come to work on aid projects and even to settle, all making for an extremely diverse population. About 40 per cent of Zambia's population is urbanised, the most densely settled areas being Lusaka and the Copperbelt.

There are seven major tribes in Zambia. Some have lived in the country for centuries whilst others are more recent settlers.

The Tonga and Ila tribes inhabit Southern Province where they have lived for perhaps 1 000 years. Their relatively peaceful existence there was greatly disrupted in the 19th century by raids from their Matabele and Lozi neighbours and then shattered in the 1950s by the flooding of their traditional lands in the Zambezi Valley under the waters of the Kariba Dam, forcing them to move to higher ground.

The Lozi are the traditional inhabitants of Barotseland based on the Barotse floodplain, which they claim extends from the Kafue to west of the Zambezi. Fiercely independent, the Lozi pledge allegiance to their king, the Litunga, and have a colourful agrarian culture that centres on the annual Kuomboka ceremony. The issue of Lozi independence from the rest of Zambia is still hotly debated.

The Luvale hail originally from the region around Lake Tanganyika whence they migrated centuries ago through Zaïre to the Zambezi watershed, conquering and assimilating smaller tribes en route. In North-western Province they are made up of the smaller Valuvale, Valuchaze, Vambunda, Vachokwe and Vaviye tribes.

The Kaonde live north and west of the Kafue River between the towns of Kaoma, Mumbwa and Solwezi. They are descended from the central African empire of the Lunda-Luba and associated with some of the earliest mining of copper.

The Lunda tribe, descended from the same empire, live in Luapula Province and North-western Province.

The Bemba are by far the most numerous people in the northern provinces and also predominate in the Copperbelt, having migrated there to work when the first mines were opened. They too have origins in the Lunda-Luba empire. They were the last tribe to make any serious stand against colonial encroachment before submitting to the British at the turn of this century.

The Ngoni, who live in Eastern Province, originated in South Africa, having fled that region during the great upheavals of the early 19th century. Arriving in what is today eastern Zambia and Malawi, they conquered and assimilated existing tribes. After their own subjugation in turn to the British Crown they declined during the 20th century and the Chewa and Tumbuka tribes gradually reasserted themselves. Although still called the Ngoni they now speak Nyanja – a language of Chewa origin.

ECONOMY

In 1990 when the Movement for Multiparty Democracy (MMD) took power in the first post-colonial election the economy of Zambia was in a dreadful state. The quasi-socialist, one-party state of the previous regime had centralised economic power by nationalising all major commerce and industry. The new government promised a radical change by decentralisation and re-privatisation of almost all sectors of the economy.

Several years after the process began, effective results have been disappointing and the country's growth rate remains negative. The biggest reason for this (see section on History) is that the new government has inherited a colossal foreign debt of US $6,6 billion, the heaviest per capita debt in the world.

The economy is based on Zambia's copper, the mining of which is the largest provider of formal employment and the biggest earner of foreign exchange. In the "humanist" wisdom of the post-colonial government the wealth of the copper mines was nationalised and for the first ten years after independence the economy developed rapidly, riding on the back of a high world copper price. In 1974 the copper price collapsed and it simply dragged the whole country down with it. Failure to detach the economy from the dependence on copper has left the country in a state of economic stagnation ever since.

Mining products are still Zambia's principal exports with copper followed to a much lesser degree by zinc, lead and cobalt. Other non-traditional exports are agricultural and horticultural products, gemstones, timber and cement. The biggest imports are crude oil, chemicals, machinery and manufactured goods.

By African standards Zambia is relatively industrialised – industry employs 60 per cent of the workforce and accounts for 24 per cent of the GDP. Agriculture has yet to realise its enormous potential. Tobacco, maize, wheat, groundnuts and beef are produced mainly by a small number of commercial farmers, the balance being the surplus produce of subsistence farmers.

Exploitation of Zambia's gemstones remains underdeveloped although the quality of Zambian emeralds is said to be unsurpassed in the world. Another legacy of the machinations of the previous government is that tourism remains a rather small contributor to the economy. As this book will show, the potential for tourism in Zambia is quite enormous and there is no reason why the tourism and agricultural sectors should not be able to put Zambia back on its feet.

Heavy reliance on depressed copper prices – which are set to fall even further – extremely high inflation, rapid population growth, corruption in many levels of the bureaucracy and a tardy conversion to the free market hold the formal sector helplessly inert between the old system and the new. It is a bleak outlook. But on the positive side, Zambia today is perhaps the most stable and pro-business country in the region. Huge yet untapped resources together with its central position, cheap labour and electricity and the economic reforms to which it has tenaciously committed itself, may still make Zambia a shining example on the continent.

2 WHAT YOU NEED TO KNOW

CLIMATE: WHEN TO VISIT

Although Zambia lies well within tropical latitudes its reasonably high altitude moderates both heat and humidity, ensuring a generally pleasant climate. The year can be divided into three seasons that determine when it is appropriate to visit the country. Between November and April, the rainy season, it is hot and wet and travel is impossible in many areas of the country, particularly many national parks where untarred roads become impassable even to four-wheel-drive vehicles. Annual rainfall varies from 700 mm in the south to over 1 200 mm (40 inches) in the north.

The rains cease in May and between then and the end of August the days are mild, but nights can be surprisingly cold. Water levels in the river valleys and floodplains recede and remote roads gradually become negotiable again.

Between September and November temperatures start rising. October is "suicide" month in the Zambezi and Luangwa valleys, very hot and dry, and the air is torpid and heavy with expectancy of the coming rains.

Obviously the best visiting times depend to some extent on the visitor's intentions. Generally the cool dry season between May and October is best. The country is most beautiful early in the season when the deciduous woodland is still green. Alas, Zambians are a nation of pyromaniacs who ritually set fire to the whole country every dry season, rendering much of the land black and ugly during the peak tourist season. Even in national parks there is a policy of burning early in the dry season to prevent the possibility of bushfires later when they will be far more destructive.

Many remote places only become accessible as the dry season progresses. Several game lodges and safari companies only open between May and October. Game viewing improves as the bush dries and thins, peaking in October when food and water resources are most limited. Fishing on the upper Zambezi is best in the dry season but on the lakes rather better in the hot months. April is a good time to visit Barotseland when the floodwaters are at their most spectacular and there's the possibility of seeing the *Kuomboka* ceremony. For bird enthusiasts the summer months offer the greatest variety although many destinations are inaccessible. It must be said, however, that the country is far, far more beautiful in the summer with vegetation so luxuriant and green that the winter months seem to belong to another country altogether. Enterprising travellers will find much to compensate for some of the impediments to travel at this time and tour operators are trying to find more activities and destinations for tourists in the "green season". Certain activities and specific destinations are best at particular times, as explained in the regional descriptions in the following chapters.

WHAT TO PACK

Clothing

Bearing in mind the climatic conditions described above, summer visitors should definitely pack rain gear. Anyone planning to visit the Victoria Falls, particularly between April and June, would do well to pack a waterproof of some sort. For all seasons one should combine light cotton clothes for warm days with something like a windcheater or bush jacket for evenings, which can be surprisingly cool. Camping in winter definitely requires provision against cold nights in the form of woollens and tracksuits. There is always plenty of sunshine, so wide-brimmed hats and loose long sleeves are a good idea. For any bush travel and game viewing neutral coloured clothes are recommended. Some safari operators distinctly frown on bright clothes as they make it very difficult to approach wildlife. White is the worst colour to wear in the bush. Bear in mind that if you do so it will disadvantage everyone else in the party as well as yourself. Tsetse flies are endemic to most national parks and they are attracted to dark colours, especially black or blue. You wear these colours on game drives and walks at risk of considerable discomfort as these pernicious little creatures can bite through all but the thickest clothing. Fortunately they are active only in daylight and such considerations need not affect one's choice of designer evening wear.

Shoes should be stout and provide protection against thorns and other hazards. After a day in boots, light strops or sandals will be a relief indeed, but don't even think about walking around barefoot, especially at night. If camping or otherwise adventuring on ones own, take a comprehensive medical kit (see section on Health precautions).

Photographic equipment

Take everything you need, with spares and plenty of film as very little can be bought locally. Binoculars are essential for game viewing as Zambian game tends to be a little more wary and standoffish than elsewhere. For the same reason big lenses are necessary for any serious game photography. Sturdy, well-cushioned camera bags are recommended to protect equipment from inevitable dust and bumping. Seal all film in plastic canisters to prevent dust and grit damaging the film during processing. Remember that excessive sun and heat can ruin film and damage equipment. Take plenty of spare batteries as you are unlikely to find replacements anywhere in Zambia. Ordinary 35 mm print film can be bought in the major centres but slide film is virtually impossible to find anywhere.

Although there are developing studios in Lusaka and Ndola it is suggested that you process your film after you return home. See section on photography in chapter 5.

Personal items

Outside Lusaka, Livingstone and the Copperbelt many toiletries and personal items such as sanitary towels or tampons, and even insect repellents, sunscreens and skin creams, are impossible to find. If planning to use small-town hotels or rest houses take your own bath plug and toilet paper.

Sporting equipment

The general rule is take your own. Fishing safari companies generally supply tackle but specialist items are often not available. Importing firearms for hunting requires special permits and an endorsement from the safari company involved.

Food and supplies

There are supermarkets with a fairly wide selection of foodstuffs in the big cities. Specialist items are unavailable outside major centres, if at all. Do not expect to find frozen meat packed in cling-wrap. However the local markets are remarkably good and depending on the season one can expect to find vegetables such as onions, sweet potatoes, tomatoes, wild spinach and rape, as well as a wide variety of fruit such as bananas, mangoes, papaws, apples, oranges and lemons. Wild berries and fruit are worth a try although many are tart. Groundnuts are abundant. All markets sell dried and sometimes fresh fish. The dried sardines or kapenta can be good as a relish but it is recommended that fresh fish be bought direct from the water's edge. Do wash all fruit and vegetables thoroughly. Hepatitis A is common and dysentery endemic. Most Zambian water is beautifully clear and potable, but it is advisable to boil it before drinking, particularly if you are near human settlements.

In most villages you will be able to buy fresh bread, baked locally and sold in portioned loaves. In addition, staples such as maize and rice are widely available. Cold drinks are available in most towns but one is usually required to drink them on the spot and return the bottle.

Mosi, the Zambian lager, deserves a special mention. Zambians are one of the largest per capita beer consuming nations in the world. Today many canned South African brands are available in major centres but Mosi, in its brown over-recycled and unlabelled bottles, is cheaper and just as good. Every fifth bottle is flat but it will be replaced without demurral. Zambian Breweries was recently taken over by South African Breweries, which may introduce changes to Zambian beer.

Small restaurants are ubiquitous and offer a standard meal of maize meal – *nshima* – and relish of kapenta or rape, sometimes with meat or chicken in addition. Try them. Such meals can be quite excellent.

Camping equipment

A few supplies are available in Lusaka, but they can be expensive so all equipment should be brought from home. Camping facilities in Zambia are unsophisticated. It is definitely not a country for caravans. The existing infrastructure does not really accommodate backpackers, who will have to carry all food and equipment into national parks and other places of interest. Tents are a good idea although not essential in the dry season. A mosquito net is recommended and simply sleeping beneath one rigged to a tree can be more comfortable than a tent on hot nights. In most national parks with big game the campsites are not enclosed, so sleeping in a tent tends to make you feel more secure during nocturnal encounters of the heavy breathing and growling kind.

If travelling into remote areas take plenty of water.

ENTRY AND CUSTOMS REGULATIONS

Citizens of most countries in the world will have no difficulty getting into Zambia provided they have a valid passport. It is not necessary for tourists to apply for visas in advance, as they can be bought on arrival at any port of entry for a nominal sum, currently US $10. Regulations have recently been relaxed for South Africans and a visa is no longer required to enter the country. Visitors from other Commonwealth countries, the Irish Republic and those states with which Zambia has visa abolition agreements, such as the Scandinavian countries and Pakistan, do not need a visa.

Visitors can import into Zambia their personal effects, photographic, sporting and camping gear and a limited quantity of beer, wine and spirits as long as such effects are declared. Foreign currency may also be imported without restriction but should be declared.

Travellers leaving the country by air should remember that there is an airport tax of US $20.

Motorists arriving in Zambia will have to obtain a customs importation permit at the point of entry and a "Motor vehicle act policy and certificate of insurance" which costs a nominal sum and is also usually available at the border post. To do this they will have to produce a valid licensing and registration certificate from the vehicle's country of origin showing engine and chassis numbers. In addition they may be required to produce proof of ownership or alternative authorisation. You may be asked to produce a valid international driver's licence. All this should be carried conveniently at hand so that these papers can be produced when required at the country's numerous roadblocks.

If you are planning to take a pet with you, a veterinary import permit must be obtained from the Director of Veterinary Services, PO Box 50060 Lusaka, and you are advised to apply a month or two in advance.

HEALTH PRECAUTIONS

Zambia does not require any specific inoculation certificates unless visitors are coming from countries such as Zaïre, Tanzania and India where they may have passed through infected areas, in which case certificates for cholera and yellow fever are desirable. However, travellers to Zambia are advised to take certain basic medical precautions. Those whose itinerary is wholly arranged and guided by registered tour operators can expect some assistance from them, but for their own comfort they should pack remedies for headaches, stomach upsets, insect bites and stings. All visitors to any part of the country in all seasons must take a course of malaria prophylaxis.

A more detailed list of health precautions follows. It is aimed at self-propelled travellers, but other visitors would do well to read it and abstract any applicable information.

Generally Zambia's health care facilities are quite good but the transport infrastructure, while considerably better than many African countries, is poorly equipped to deal with life-threatening emergencies in remote places. Distances are great while roads and communication are poor, so considerable delays can be expected between accidents and hospitalisation or treatment. The major centres have quite reasonable hospitals and rural clinics are fairly abundant. These are not always adequately staffed, however, and stricken travellers should head straight for the nearest mission hospital, of which a good network exists right across the country. Missions often have an expatriate doctor in attendance as well as radio communication and sometimes even their own aircraft to deal with extreme emergencies.

Taking out medical insurance with one of several medical insurance companies who will "casevac" emergency patients to South Africa or Europe is a sensible precaution.

A comprehensive medical kit is essential for self-propelled travellers going to remote places. This should include at least the following: Alleviants for diarrhoea and vomiting, such as Imodium and Valoid. Oral rehydration salts are an essential part of a medical kit. Good painkillers. A few rolls of crêpe bandage for severe lacerations and to use as a pressure bandage in the case of snakebite. Assorted stretch fabric plasters. Paraffin gauze dressing for burns, the most likely and least pleasant of camping injuries. A disinfectant such as Mercurochrome. Antiseptic and antihistamine creams.

Some knowledge of first aid is necessary. In addition the wilderness traveller might consider taking a snakebite kit, although antivenom should only be used when all other options for treatment have failed. Generally application of a crêpe bandage, wrapping it around the entire affected limb to close down the lymphatic system, and evacuation to hospital should be the preferred option. In view of the prevalence of Aids and hepatitis B it is probably sensible to take a small supply of one's own needles, although going to the extent of carrying quantities of one's own dehydrated blood is recommended only to the paranoid.

Possible illness, prevention, diagnosis and action

Malaria

The threat of malaria cannot be overemphasised. If you do not take appropriate prophylactics you will almost certainly come down with the disease and if you are then not properly diagnosed and treated you might die. Malaria is on the increase in Africa. Chloroquin-resistant mosquitoes, against which some traditional prophylactics are no longer effective, are prevalent in Zambia.

Reputable medical advice should be sought before your trip. Generally a combined course of chloroquin and non-chloroquin based pills is advised. Take as prescribed and in particular be sure to see out the full course after leaving the malaria-infected area as the parasite remains in the bloodstream for a considerable time.

Summer is a particularly high-risk period, whereas the dry season is less risky and visitors might consider this when planning a visit to Zambia. The river valleys and swamp areas carry a greater risk, but don't take chances; consider the whole country malaria-prone at all times of the year.

The best protection against malaria is to take steps to avoid being bitten. Mosquitoes are most active in the early evening and very early morning. Wear long sleeves, long trousers and socks, and apply mosquito repellent to any exposed skin. If venturing into swampy terrain, take these precautions in the day as well. Sleep under a mosquito net. Almost all lodges supply them, but many urban hotels do not. It is most unlikely that you will avoid being bitten entirely, so don't for a moment consider that taking such precautions means you can skip the malaria tablets.

Symptoms: Not all mosquitoes carry malaria. The malaria parasite usually takes two weeks to manifest itself. Symptoms are very varied and sometimes difficult to diagnose. Unfortunately prophylactics exacerbate the problem by suppressing the parasite and masking symptoms. Reasons for alarm are severe headaches, diarrhoea and vomiting, and flu-like symptoms progressing to fever. As the disease takes hold victims become delirious. In the case of cerebral malaria death can follow within a week.

Treatment: If you suspect malaria consult a doctor immediately. In the absence of an alternative diagnosis treat for malaria anyway. Early treatment will ensure a rapid recovery; various medicines are prescribed which should clear the parasite within a week, leaving only mild side-effects. Extra special care should be taken by visitors leaving Africa directly after being in a malaria area as doctors not accustomed to tropical diseases may misdiagnose the disease. If in doubt it is wise to tell the doctor that you suspect malaria, and consult a specialist in tropical diseases. If no symptoms have manifested eight weeks after leaving a malaria area you should be in the clear.

Tickbite fever

Although not usually fatal this is a very unpleasant disease against which there are no prophylactics. Only some ticks carry the disease, so if you are bitten it doesn't mean you will automatically fall ill. To avoid being bitten wear long trousers and socks and apply an insect repellent to the line of your trouser hem. After walking in the bush and especially thick grass inspect your whole body with minute attention. The tiny ticks are the most dangerous. Don't simply pull ticks out as their heads may be left behind and they can eventually cause a nasty sore. Smear them with Vaseline or paraffin which will suffocate them and cause them to loosen their hold, then remove them by grabbing the head, not the body, with tweezers.

Treatment is possible with tetracyclines. Sickness may cause unpleasant delirium but the disease is readily curable.

Sleeping sickness

Much of Zambia is still inhabited by tsetse flies, the carriers of *trypanasomiasis*, which causes this chronic illness. Wooded escarpments and the major river valleys where there is game harbour hordes of these tenacious creatures which, if attracted by movement, will zoom in and inflict a most painful bite. The insect looks rather like a horsefly. It is extremely tough and will not succumb to even quite a hard swat. The tsetse fly has an awesome proboscis which can penetrate the toughest clothing and against which repellents are quite ineffectual. Tsetse flies are only active during daylight hours and particularly attracted to dark colours and movement. They are incapable of flying far from trees so when totally exasperated by them head for a wide open space and keep still. Wear baggy, light-coloured clothing.

Only the tiniest fraction of bites result in sleeping sickness in human beings. Cattle succumb far more easily. Inhabitants of infected areas are bitten all the time and very few ever get the disease. Nowadays the illness is readily curable and not life-threatening. Tsetse flies can, however, make walking or driving in heavily infected areas most unpleasant. A wise precaution if planning to drive into affected areas is to pack some pieces of fly screen that can then be taped to the vehicle's windows to keep the pests at bay.

Do remember that the tsetse fly has earned a reputation as the single greatest protector of wildlife on the continent because it prevents human encroachment in so many areas.

Rabies

This very nasty and always fatal disease is carried particularly by small carnivores and domestic dogs and cats. Beware of "tame" looking wild animals such as jackals and mongooses as well as aggressive dogs and cats. If bitten by a suspect animal consult a doctor immediately. It is possible to be inoculated against rabies but once the disease has taken hold a dreadful death is ensured. If you are going to be travelling rough for some length of time in Africa a rabies inoculation is a good idea.

Bilharzia

This parasite is carried by a snail that inhabits still water at the edges of lakes and rivers, particularly near human settlement. Few rivers in Zambia can be guaranteed free of bilharzia, so care should be taken when swimming. If you do swim, you stand an even better chance of being eaten by a crocodile than of catching bilharzia, so there's every good reason to remain on dry land. If you still decide to take the plunge and emerge alive, dry yourself vigorously to remove any larvae that may have remained on your skin.

Symptoms of bilharzia include drowsiness, loss of vigour and eventually blood in both urine and stools. The disease is easily cured.

Hepatitis

This is a viral disease that causes jaundice and liver complaints. The more common form is hepatitis A, which is carried by water and food contaminated with human excrement. Avoid drinking water from streams and ponds near human settlements without boiling it vigorously for ten minutes beforehand. Wash vegetables very thoroughly and preferably peel and cook them before eating.

Hepatitis B is lethal and transferred by blood contact, so safe sex and sterilised needles are precautions against it.

Diarrhoea and dysentery

Dysentery is an amoebic infection of the intestine. Its symptom is very severe diarrhoea. Few things ruin a holiday as quickly as a bad case of diarrhoea. The cause is usually contaminated water and food. Be sure to wash food bought in local markets. If it looks dubious avoid it. Zambia is fortunate to be amply coursed with rivers of wonderful clear water, but be careful. As a rule, always boil drinking water thoroughly. Do not take it for granted that water in the major centres is drinkable. Lusaka water particularly is considered dubious and unless you have a cast-iron stomach you would do better to drink bottled or boiled liquids.

At the same time travellers should consider that the greater the resistance built up by the body, the less the likelihood of falling ill. Those who painstakingly avoid anything but the most sterilised of foods are bound to slip up somewhere and then infection is all the more likely. Eat and drink with caution but, particularly if your visit is a lengthy one, let your system get as used to local conditions as possible.

Do have a supply of anti-diarrhoea tablets at hand and, most importantly, after a diarrhoea attack drink plenty of liquids and take oral rehydration salts. Diarrhoea causes dehydration and dehydration can end in death. If one or two tablets do not stop diarrhoea, do not continue with them – rather consult a doctor as soon as possible.

Other possibilities

Putsi fly is a horrible little creature that lays its eggs on wet fabric. After washing clothes be sure to iron them thoroughly. If putsi fly eggs survive in clothes the larvae hatch in contact with warm skin and immediately burrow into the skin, causing a small boil-like bump with a black centre. If left alone they eventually re-emerge as flies. To remove maggots once infected, apply grease to the affected area which will prevent the larvae from breathing. If it does not come out on its own, apply pressure to force it out.

The flies themselves resemble tsetse flies and inflict an unpleasant and stinging bite by diving down shirt fronts or other openings in clothing. They are not, however, all that common and less prevalent in the dry season.

Scorpions can be divided into two kinds. The large black ones have comparatively big pincers, and a sting from one of these is not terribly serious. Small brown ones have quite small pincers. These are more poisonous and a sting can cause severe swelling and discomfort but rarely death. Treat symptomatically.

If the victim starts showing severe symptoms seek medical attention. If you shake out your shoes before putting them on each morning a scorpion sting is unlikely.

Snakes are common all over the country. Only a small number of species are poisonous. Generally they bite only under extreme provocation. Very few people are bitten and of those very few die. Nevertheless snakebite is extremely traumatic and you should take every precaution against it. Proceed warily when walking in the bush. Wear long trousers and boots. Be careful particularly after sunset when most snakes are active and especially when collecting firewood. Wear shoes all the time. In a close encounter with a snake don't panic – walk away quietly. Don't pick up seemingly dead snakes.

Although not all bites, even from poisonous snakes, result in poisoning, it is natural to fear the worst. Different snakes provoke different symptoms: An adder or cobra bite causes immediate burning pain followed by swelling. Mamba bites quickly result in dizziness and breathing difficulty. Treesnakes and twig snakes provoke terrible headaches some hours after the bite, followed by bleeding from cuts and mucous membranes, then internal haemorrhaging.

Unaccompanied travellers into the bush would do well to carry a snake guidebook and find out in advance how to deal with snakebite. The following are just a few first aid tips: Don't panic but move quickly to calm the victim. The victim should move as little as possible. Immediately apply a pressure bandage to the bitten area and preferably wind it firmly round the entire limb. The aim of this is to immobilise the lymphatic system. Cutting off the blood supply with a tourniquet can do irreparable tissue damage. Suction on the bite wound may help if it is done immediately, preferably with a suction device.

Unprotected suction by mouth may poison the sucker if they have any mouth lesions. Don't try to kill the snake which may very well lead to another bite, but if it's definitely dead take it with you to aid identification. Rush the victim to hospital, but try to keep him as still as possible.

Do not inject serum without proper medical supervision unless help is not at hand and it is clear that death will otherwise result.

Certain cobras spit venom, some as far as 2,5 m. Venom that lands on skin will do no harm but if any gets in your eyes terrible burning and swelling will result, which if not treated may cause blindness. Rinse the eyes immediately with whatever harmless liquid comes to hand: water, milk, cold drink or beer. If you have absolutely nothing else available even urine will help. Then get medical attention as soon as possible. It may be necessary to rinse the eyes with serum diluted 1:9 in water.

Crocodiles abound in Zambian rivers and lakes and even the shallowest and most peaceful-looking stretch of water may conceal a hungry reptile. So be careful when drawing water and preferably don't swim. The locals usually know whether waters are safe. There are many stories about people who thought there wasn't a croc for miles around, only to become a crocodillic banquet five minutes later!

Aids is today a bigger killer by far than all of the above combined. Aids is absolutely rife in Zambia, especially along the trucking routes. A drive out to the main cemetery on Leopard's Hill Road in Lusaka to count the number of funerals a day serves as a sobering reminder that sexual contact with anyone you do not know very well indeed is tantamount to signing a death warrant. Today even in Zambia Aids awareness is widespread so it needs little elaboration.

Adventurous travellers to places like Zambia should take condoms. Special Aids kits with plasma, syringes, needles, etc. are available. Short of succumbing to total paranoia it is probably sensible to pack your own syringes and needles and for self-propelled travellers to take surgical gloves which, if nothing else, could make them less squeamish about helping out at someone else's accident.

CURRENCY AND BANKS

The Zambian monetary unit is the kwacha and 1 kwacha is officially divided into 100 ngwee, but recent inflation has so diminished the value of the kwacha that the smaller currency unit has all but fallen away. Some public telephones still require ngwee coins, which are best purchased in the local post office and then fed into the phone in large numbers to get a few seconds of call time.

Kwacha are issued in K500, K100, K50 and K20 notes. A K10 coin has recently been issued. Even the largest units have to be carried around in great wads to buy anything. In January 1994 1 US dollar was worth K675 and 1 South African rand could buy K185. Prices generally are not outrageous. A beer in a hotel bar, for example, cost between K500 and K1 000 in 1994. Inflation is still high and although the kwacha has recently rallied against foreign currencies, it can be expected to continue declining in value for some time yet.

All restrictions on foreign currency dealing have been lifted. You can change currency over the counter in any bank. In recent years the black market was legalised and made official by the creation of bureaus de change. With the lifting of all remaining restrictions even these are expected to fall away.

Changing money on the street is not illegal, but it is unwise as you are likely to be ripped off. If banks are closed try shops, hotels or even petrol station attendants, who will not run away when you have handed over your side of the bargain. Banks are open between 08:15 and 14:30 or 15:00 on weekdays and until 11:00 on Saturdays. Almost every town will have at least one bank where money can be changed during those hours. In some rural banks the process can however be painfully slow.

PUBLIC HOLIDAYS

1 January – New Year's Day

19 March – Youth Day

March/April – Good Friday

March/April – Holy Saturday

1 May – Labour Day

25 May – African Freedom Day

First Monday in July – Heroes' Day

First Tuesday in July – Unity Day

First Monday in August – Farmers' Day

24 October – Independence Day

25 December – Christmas Day

TIME

It is worth noting that Zambians unilaterally use the 24-hour clock. To refer, for example, to two o'clock in the afternoon will cause confusion if not total incomprehension. Rather say, "14 hours" or simply, "I will meet you at 14".

LANGUAGE

No less than 73 different dialects are spoken in Zambia. Thankfully, though, English is the official language and is spoken throughout the country. Even in remote areas it is rare to find a village where no one speaks any English. But for those situations where communication without recourse to English is necessary, such as asking directions, and indeed simply as a politeness, it may be helpful to know a few ice-breaking or emergency phrases in the major local languages. There are seven of these in the country; they are classified as semi-official languages and they are generally spoken in the different regions outlined below.

Bemba is possibly the largest indigenous language and is spoken both on the Copperbelt and throughout Northern Province.

Kaonde is spoken widely in the region north-west of Lusaka, particularly around the northern Kafue and in the districts of Kasempa and Solwezi.

Lozi is a Sotho-based language and it is spoken all over Western Province, especially around Mongu.

Lunda is predominantly spoken in north-western Zambia around Mwinilunga.

Luvale is spoken in north-western Zambia, particularly between Lukulu, Kabompo and Chavuma.

Nyanja, the language of the Ngoni people, is generally spoken from Lusaka eastwards, particularly in the eastern region. The Ngoni still speak their original Ndebele-like language on ceremonial occasions.

Tonga is spoken in Southern Province between Chirundu and the Victoria Falls.

Here is a brief guide to greetings and emergency phrases in each language.

Bemba

- Good morning sir/madam.
  Mwashibukeru mukwai. (Pronounced m'kwai.)
  Reply:
  Eya mukwai.
- Good afternoon.
  Mutende mukwai.

Reply:
Endita mukwai.

- Good evening.
Cungulopo mukwai.

Reply:
Eya mukwai.

- If greeting a child or close friend you may use the greeting *Uli shani?* (How are you?)

Reply:
Ndifye bwino. (I am alright/ok.)

- I need a doctor.
Ndefwaya dokota.

- He/she is over there.
Ulya ali palya.

- Where is the bus station?
Nga basi sitesheni ilikwi? (Note anglicism.)

- It is over there.
Ili apo.

Kaonde

- Good morning sir or madam. (How are you?)
Mwabuuka mwane.

Reply:
Ee mwane kana nweba. (I am fine – and you?)

- If greeting a child or friend:
Wabuuka.

- I need a doctor.
Mbena kukeba dokota.

- He or she is over there.
Uji kokwa.

- Where is the passport office?
Pasipoti ofesi ijipi?

- It is on Cairo Road.
Pasipoti ofesi iji ma Cairo road.

- Where is the bus station?
Nga kitesheyi kya ma basi kijipi?

Lozi

- Good morning sir or madam.
  Mwazuha.
- If greeting a child or friend:
  Wazuha.

  Reply:
  Eni sha.
- How are you?
  Muzuhile cwani?
- I am fine; and you?
  Batili nizuhile hande; nimina mucwani?.
- I am fine too.
  Batili nazuha.
- I need a doctor.
  Nibata dokota.
- The doctor is over there.
  Dokota winzi fo.
- Where is the bus station?
  Ikanti sitesheni ya basi ikai?
- It is not far.
  Inzi fakaufi.
- It is quite far.
  Inzi kwaule.
- Where is the passport office?
  Kanti pasipoti ofesi ikai?
- It is on Cairo Road.
  Inzi mwa Cairo Road.

Lunda

- Good morning.
  Handemi mwani.
- How are you?
  Mundi wahi mwani.
- I am looking for a doctor.
  Nina kukena kudi ndontolo kudi.

- Where is the bus station?
  Bus station idi kundi kuno?
- Which road goes to the passport office?
  Jila yakuya ku passport office indi kundi?

Luvale

- Good morning.
  Muli ngadu lilu.
- How are you?
  Numa yoyo mwane?
- I am looking for a doctor.
  Nguna kutonda kuli ndontolo kuli.
- Where is the bus station?
  Bus station ya twa mina kuli kuno?
- Which road goes to the passport office?
  Ngulweze uko jila yakuya ku passport office?

Nyanja

- How are you this morning?
  Mwauka bwanji? (Again, if spoken to a minor or good friend the respectful prefix "M-" can be dropped.)
  Mulibwanji? is acceptable as a daily greeting.
- I am fine.
  Ndili bwino.
- I need a doctor.
  Ndifuna Dotolo.
- The doctor is over there.
  Dotolo ali kuja.
- Where is the bus station?
  Nanga basi sitesheni ilikuti?
- Which road goes to the passport office?
  Ndi iti njila yaku pasipoti ofesi?
- It is called Cairo Road.
  Icedwa Cairo Road.

Tonga

- Good morning sir/madam.
  Mwabuka. (Simply *wabuka* to inferior or friend.)
- I'm fine; and how are you?
  Ndi kabolu; muli buti?
- I need a doctor.
  Ndiyanda dokota.
- The doctor is over there.
  Dokota ali awa.
- Where is the bus station?
  Basi siteshoni ili kuli?
- Where is the passport office?
  Pasipoti ofesi ili ali?
- It is on Cairo Road.
  Mulaijana mu Cairo Road.

SECURITY

There is a popular misconception that Zambia is a grand den of thieves with armed thugs and malcontents waiting behind every bush and around every corner to pounce on unsuspecting tourists. Curiously, it is a perception fostered by Zambians themselves. And it is nonsense. Zambia is one of the safest countries on the continent to travel in. That is, of course, a qualified statement and Zambia is far from being crime-free. Armed car theft occurs regularly in Lusaka and along sections of the Zaïrean border in the vicinity of the Copperbelt. However, such incidents are far less common than in Johannesburg, for example. Generally large, new and anonymous-looking four-wheel-drives will be the targets. Always lock your vehicles and in Lusaka or crowded places keep an eye on the car when parking for a length of time. Petty theft will take place if it is invited. Lock hotel rooms and leave valuables in the hotel safe. Don't carry all your money in the same pocket or bag.

   Look confident and keep your wits about you. In short, take the same reasonable precautions that you would when travelling anywhere in the world.

SUGGESTED READING

Zambia has not featured in travel writing or popular fiction in the same way that east and southern Africa have. But for those interested in knowing more about the country than this book can provide, here are some suggestions. If you read nothing else, Mike Main's *Zambezi, Journey of a River* (Southern Books, South Africa, 1990) is essential. Used as source material for this book, this is a fascinating combination of detail, anecdote and adventure about the river and the region it passes through. The National Heritage Conservation Commission of Zambia has published a guide book to the National Monuments of Zambia by D W Phillipson which is an indispensable guide to places of historical or particularly scenic interest. Many have been included in these pages but the booklet includes several places we have not mentioned and has a map giving their location. It can be bought from the commission offices in Livingstone.

Other books on Zambia are less contemporary and more difficult to get hold of. *Generation of Men: The European Pioneers of Northern Rhodesia* (Stuart Manning, Salisbury, 1965) by W V Brelsford, is an account of some of the pioneers, explorers, characters and downright brigands who came into the territory during the early colonial era. There are bound volumes of *The Occasional Papers of the Rhodes-Livingstone Museum* and *The Northern Rhodesia Journal*, both dating from the pre-independence era and filled with scientific information and interesting esoterica from those days. There are two books on the Fisher family of Kalene Hill which give an account of pioneer missionary days in western Zambia, *Ndotulu* by W S Fisher and J Hoyte, and *Nswana – The Heir* by Monica Fisher. The former is out of print but the latter is available in Lusaka bookshops. Lastly, don't leave home without good bird books and other wildlife field guides. And remember that for many species found in Zambia southern African books are insufficient, so supplement with central and east African books.

3 HOW TO GET TO ZAMBIA

BY AIR

Zambia's main international airport lies just outside Lusaka and most incoming international flights land there. There is an international airport at Livingstone, but direct flights there tend to be erratic and mostly confined to charters.

Aero Zambia fly Lusaka-Johannesburg Monday, Tuesday, Friday; Johannesburg-Lusaka Monday, Tuesday, Saturday; Nairobi-Lusaka Tuesdays and Thursdays returning Mondays and Thursdays; to and from Dar-es-salaam on Thursdays; Harare-Lusaka-Harare Wednesday, Friday and Sunday. Aero Zambia do not fly to Livingstone. The airline is planning flights to and from Kinshasa, Luanda, Entebbe, Maputo and Dubai shortly.

A few other airlines land at Lusaka, including British Airways and Air France from Europe. South African Airways fly twice weekly to and from Johannesburg. Aeroflot, Angola Airlines, Air Namibia, Royal Swazi Air, Air Tanzania, Air Zaire and Air Zimbabwe all land at Lusaka.

BY RAIL

The only regular passenger train service in and out of Zambia is the Tanzania-Zambia Railway, known as the Tazara express, which runs once a week between Dar es Salaam in Tanzania and Kapiri Mposhi in Zambia and back again. Only the express goes the whole way with customs and immigration facilities done on board. But it is also possible to catch ordinary trains running twice weekly in either direction that connect at but do not cross the border. The border between Tunduma and Nakonde used to be one of the most infamous border crossings in Africa. Today it is not exactly trouble-free, but blame for this has shifted from the Zambian side, where officials are courteous, to the Tanzanian side where bribery and corruption are becoming rife. Play it straight and you will be okay. The only complication is that Tazara runs to and from Kapiri Mposhi, so a connection must be made with the regular service between Livingstone, Lusaka and Kitwe. The two trains do not connect directly, however. Either you have to spend a night and the better part of a day in Kapiri, which is not a particularly salubrious town, or hitchhike or take a bus between there and Lusaka. There is a regular hourly bus service between the two places.

Theoretically it would also be possible to take trains to the two other border points connected by rail in Zambia: Livingstone opposite Victoria Falls in Zimbabwe, and Ndola which is connected by rail to Lubumbashi in Zaïre. There do not, however, appear to be regular passenger services connecting the border posts in those countries. A tradition has started of an annual trip on a highly exclusive nostalgic steam train from South Africa through Zimbabwe and Zambia to Dar es Salaam. Contact Rovos Rail in South Africa for details.

BY BUS

There is a regular bus service between Lusaka and Harare in Zimbabwe via Chirundu. The United Bus Company of Zambia, UBZ, runs between the two cities every day of the week except Sunday. It is wise to book in advance as this service is very popular.

For travellers from South Africa there is an equally regular coach service between Johannesburg and Harare. Or you could take a coach to Bulawayo and a bus from there to Victoria Falls before crossing to Livingstone in Zambia on foot (necessitating a 10-km hitch into town).

From Malawi there is a private bus company that runs all the way between Lilongwe and Lusaka. Or you can take the national bus companies to and from the border through Chipata. From Tanzania there are no direct buses but national buses to and from the border at Tunduma-Nakonde. From Zaïre there is again no direct coach service but you can take buses or hitchhike with a choice of two borders: Either between Chililabombwe and Kasumbelesa or between Mufulira and Mokambo. The whole border area is notorious for bandits and Zaïrean officials are far from incorruptible, so keep your wits about you. Chingola is fairly safe but either way you are advised to proceed straight through to Kitwe or Ndola.

BY BOAT

The ferries on Lake Tanganyika connect the Zambian "port" of Mpulungu with Kigoma in Tanzania and Bujumbura in Burundi. The Tanzania Railways Corporation runs two boats, the MV *Liemba* and the MV *Mwongozo*. The *Mwongozo* only serves Tanzanian towns but the

Liemba runs weekly between the three countries. The *Liemba* is an ancient vessel with an interesting history. It was originally named the *Graf von Goetzn* and saw service under the Germans in the First World War. To avert capture by the British it was eventually scuttled but in 1927 the British raised it and, thanks to the Germans who had greased the boat from top to bottom before sinking it, the renamed *Liemba* has plied the lake ever since. The TRC agents for the ferry in Zambia are Cosy Enterprises Ltd, with booking offices in Mpulungu and Lusaka. The *Liemba* has six first-class cabins, each with two beds, 12 2nd-class with four bunks in each and a 3rd-class lower deck. Expect to pay about US $75 for 1st class, $60 for 2nd class and $35 for 3rd class.

BY MOTOR CAR

There are several ways to get into Zambia in your own vehicle. Visitors coming up from South Africa can choose between three routes through Zimbabwe, one through Botswana and one through Namibia. The most direct route to Lusaka is to go through Harare and cross the border at Chirundu. It is a good tar road with fuel and facilities at regular intervals the whole way.

From Harare it is also possible to go via Kariba crossing the border over the dam wall. Alternatively take the Bulawayo road past Hwange Game Reserve to Victoria Falls, possibly the nicest stretch of road in all Africa, then cross over the Victoria Falls Bridge which, as a fitting culmination of that road, is surely one of the world's great frontiers.

A popular route from South Africa is to go through Botswana, which obviates the expense of a Zimbabwe visa. But any tourists who intend taking a boat to Zambia should note that Botswana expressly forbids the transit of any kind of boat through its territory without the authority of the Department of Water Affairs in Gaborone. Proceed via Francistown and Nata, and then up the Pandamatenga road to Kazungula. It's all tar and from Nata onwards it is a beautiful route. A stopover in the spectacular Chobe National Park is possible before you either cross the border by ferry directly at Kazungula or proceed into Zimbabwe to the Victoria Falls to cross the border there. Of course the latter will necessitate buying a Zimbabwe visa, but affords travellers the chance of seeing game, especially elephant, on the road to Victoria Falls.

Only travellers specifically heading for the upper Zambezi and Barotseland are recommended to take the Namibian route and cross into

Zambia at Katima Mulilo. Even if coming from central Namibia, if you are heading for Livingstone you are advised to go through Botswana and cross on the Kazungula ferry or proceed all the way into Zimbabwe and over the border at the Falls. The reason for this is, as fully described in chapter 8, that the road from Katima Mulilo to Livingstone in Zambia is indescribably bad, and in addition you will have to pay R60 to cross on the Sesheke ferry.

It is assumed that the route through Mozambique will remain little travelled for a while yet. You have to go through Zimbabwe anyway and into Mozambique at Tete. Once in Zambia, having crossed the border at Mlolo, you join the Great East Road at Katete, within easy striking distance of the South Luangwa.

From Malawi the only tar route and the usual way is to go from Lilongwe to Chipata, again within striking distance of the South Luangwa and about 570 km from Lusaka. There are three other points of entry in northern Malawi, two off the Nyika Plateau which are described in the chapter on eastern Zambia and only recommended if you particularly want to go from there to the Luangwa Valley or take a shortcut to northern Zambia via Isoka. The third at Chitipa is really used as a route up to Tanzania, as it runs for about 50 km through Zambia to the Tanzanian border at Tunduma.

From Tanzania and east Africa, motorists can choose between crossing the border at Tunduma, which is the most direct route from Dar es Salaam and Dodoma, or boarding the Lake Tanganyika Ferry, the MV *Liemba* at Kigoma, possibly the most direct route from Kenya and Uganda, or boarding at Bujumbura in Burundi. The ferry docks at Mpulungu in Zambia.

Travellers coming south from Zaïre will take the road from Lubumbashi to Chingola and the Copperbelt. It is not a pleasant frontier with bandits on either side of the border although the Zambians stepped up security in the region after a spate of car hijackings, including one of a cabinet minister.

At the moment the Angolan frontiers do not really bear speaking about, as most fall within territory not controlled by the Angolan government. Eventually it may be possible to cross at Jimbe Bridge right in the north-west corner of Zambia.

4 GETTING AROUND

It is assumed that tourists to Zambia will fall into one of the three following groups:

- Those travelling by air and under the aegis of organised tours and safaris.
- Those travelling in their own vehicle (preferably, but not necessarily, a four-wheel-drive).
- "Backpackers" travelling by means of public transport, hitchhiking or on bicycles.

BY AIR

Most major towns in Zambia have airstrips but internal commercial air travel is fairly limited. Aero Zambia, the national airline, has been plagued by inefficiency, with delays and cancellations more the rule than the exception. The Zambian Government is intervening to remedy the state of affairs. Aero Zambia has recently undergone some restructuring, and visitors should check the availability and time of their flights carefully. In addition to the national airline there are charter companies which will land on any registered strip. Some of these are listed in Chapter 13. There are regular flights between Lusaka and Ndola in the Copperbelt. For details of other towns around the country that can be reached by private charter planes, travellers should contact one of the private charter companies.

ORGANISED TOURS AND SAFARIS

For the uninitiated, without their own vehicle and whose interest lies mainly in seeing the country's wildlife, this is the hassle-free option. A number of safari and tour operators operate out of Lusaka and Livingstone or have bases in and around the major game reserves. Prices are very competitive when compared with those of operators elsewhere in southern or east Africa. Chapter 13 gives a complete list of these operators, their addresses and the regions in which they specialise. The majority run safaris to either the South Luangwa National Park or the Kafue National Park or specialise in trips and adventures on the Zambezi River. There are companies that run specialist safaris to other areas and some companies will tailor trips to clients' specific interests. Zambia's recent conversion to a free-market economy has resulted in a massive increase in the number of tour operators licensed in the country. Most of those in existence at the time of writing are listed in chapter 13, but it is likely that others will have come into being thereafter, so consult the travel agencies or the Zambian National Tourist Board, or address enquiries to the Tour Operators Association of Zambia, Amandra House, Ben Bella Road, Lusaka, Box 36655, Lusaka.

BY TRAIN

Zambia's rail network is limited to a single line from Livingstone to Lusaka and thence north to Kapiri Mposhi where it forks, one branch proceeding through the Copperbelt to Zaïre and the other, the famous Tanzania-Zambia Railway (Tazara), going north-east via Mpika and Kasama to Tunduma and Tanzania, where it ends ultimately in Dar es Salaam. Travellers can choose between sleeper, standard and economy rates on local trains or 1st, 2nd and 3rd class on Tazara.

There is a daily service that runs from Livingstone through Lusaka to Kitwe via Kapiri Mposhi and in the opposite direction. Slow and a little erratic, the trains take about 12 hours between Livingstone and Lusaka and the same again to the Copperbelt. Rates in kwacha are the equivalent of about US $4 for a sleeper or $2 economy between each city. Travellers wishing to take Tazara to Dar es Salaam should note that the train leaves from Kapiri Mposhi and it does not connect with the normal north- or southbound service, necessitating an overnight stop and a day's wait in Kapiri. The weekly train normally departs at 18:00, so it would be possible to take a bus to or from Kapiri on the same day. Tazara must be booked at least one week in advance. Rates are approximately US $40 1st class, $26 2nd class and $12 if you have the sang-froid to brave 3rd class.

BY BUS

Buses are the main means of inter-city transport in Zambia and cover an extensive network throughout the country. The main carrier is the United Bus Company of Zambia, UBZ, but other lines operate on some routes. For backpackers this is the safest and most inexpensive way of getting around the country. Most routes are covered daily and the major ones several times daily. Other than the major intercity lines, buses tend not to follow strict schedules, rather departing once they are full. It's as well therefore to arrive early on prospective dates of departure. Buses are reasonably reliable, although subject to many delays en route at roadblocks and pick-up points. Be aware of, if not necessarily deterred by, incidents such as one witnessed by the authors where a bus broke down on a country road and two weeks later the hapless passengers were still encamped beside the vehicle, dependent on nearby villages and foraging in the bush for food. Of course victims of such a mishap with a little spare cash could simply hitchhike on or flag down the next passing bus.

BY BOAT

On certain waterways boat travel is a delightful way of getting around. Lake Kariba has a ferry between Siavonga and Sinazongwe. During the high-water season there's a post boat between major towns in Barotseland. Motor launches are definitely the quickest way around Lake Tanganyika and there are large ferries plying between countries on the lake, for details of which see chapter 3. The slow but regular canoe traffic between villages on all navigable Zambian rivers is used by the locals but is yet to be explored as a means of travel for intrepid tourists. Ferries and pontoons are to be found all over the country. The motorised ferries on the Zambezi charge a fortune to transport foreign vehicles; currently about US $25, but the ubiquitous hand powered pontoons on smaller rivers are free. See regional routes for more details.

HITCHHIKING

Zambia's tourist infrastructure is not well adapted to backpackers, but nevertheless it is by no means impossible to tour the country in this way. As has been mentioned elsewhere Zambians are tremendously courteous and helpful by nature, so lifts will be forthcoming, but you should expect to pay something and it may save difficulty later if a fee is agreed on at the outset. Major routes have regular but certainly not prolific traffic, mostly consisting of very weary looking old Land Rovers limping along like war veterans under loads of quite grotesque proportions. Overloading is not in the Zambian vocabulary and hikers are assured of plenty of company on their journey. Truckers are usually a reliable source of lifts if approached while stationary – these juggernauts stop for nothing once they get going. Do not expect much traffic along secondary roads. The biggest drawback to hitchhiking in Zambia is that there are sometimes large distances to be covered between major roads and destinations in game parks or other attractions, so good walking shoes and/or no end of patience may be considered essential equipment.

IN YOUR OWN VEHICLE

The majority of Zambia's roads are negotiable in an ordinary car and four-wheel-drive is recommended mostly to cope with the wear and tear of the potholes and bumps on roads which have to date been ill maintained. However minor roads, particularly in game parks, will occasionally present obstacles such as gullies and riverbeds that do necessitate four-wheel-drive. Roads in western Zambia are sometimes very sandy and four-wheel-drive is definitely recommended for this region. In the rainy season minor roads can be hazardous even in four-wheel-drive and some, where there's black clay "cotton soil", simply not negotiable at all.

There's a hoary old chestnut that goes: How do you tell a drunk driver in Zambia? The answer is that he is the one who drives straight down the road. Beware complacency and high speed on tar roads, as even apparently good surfaces can suddenly collapse into bone and metal-shattering craters. Note too that particularly buses and trucks negotiate these craters not by slowing down but by careening all over the road, yielding only to bigger buses or trucks. We cannot recommend more strongly that whatever car you drive – drive slowly and even very slowly where roads deteriorate if you wish to take your vehicle home in the same condition that it first entered the territory. A good rule of thumb would be to not travel in excess of 300 kilometres per day

There are a number of car hire companies in Zambia which operate from the main cities. Some also offer chauffeurs and four-wheel-drive vehicles. These are listed in detail in chapter 13.

5 WHAT TO DO

MOTOR TOURING AND EXPLORING

There is no doubt that driving in your own, preferably a four-wheel-drive vehicle, is the best way to see the country. This is really what this book is about and will be dealt with in the following chapters on the regions. Do note the section on getting around by car in chapter 4, and read the section on driving tips and motor spares in chapter 13.

NATIONAL PARKS AND GAME VIEWING

Most tourists to Zambia will be coming to visit the country's game reserves. From the early days of European exploration the African interior north of the Zambezi was known for its vast herds of game, particularly elephant, and the ivory trade has existed since time immemorial. In some areas, particularly the Lozi Kingdom of Barotseland, traditional law controlled exploitation of wildlife resources. However, increasing trade competition toward the end of the 19th century precipitated alarming over-exploitation, especially of ivory, and at the beginning of this century the newly arrived colonial administrations introduced regulations to control hunting. From these regulations emerged the first game reserves as well as elephant control officers whose job it was to shoot marauding animals, but who became in fact the proto-conservationists that began to set aside wilderness areas for game preservation. At first such reserves were used for hunting safaris followed by the introduction of photographic and walking safaris. The walking safari, which is so popular in Africa today, may be said to have been pioneered in the Luangwa Valley. Protection for the first three-quarters of the century saw game numbers increase enormously. For example, in the Luangwa Valley where they had been practically wiped out at the beginning of the century, there were almost 100 000 elephants and several thousand black rhino by 1970.

Like almost every thing else under the Kaunda government these reserves, some amongst the most famous big-game areas on the continent, were nationalised and the majority proclaimed "National Parks" in the 1970s. Sadly, with the introduction of vast quantities of automatic rifles into the country as that government took several of the subcontinent's liberation movements under its wing, poaching assumed greater proportions than ever before.

Coupled with an abrogation of responsibility and downright corruption by the government, a wholesale slaughter was begun that in little more than a decade wiped out 80 per cent of the country's game populations. The hundreds of thousands of elephants were reduced to a total population of perhaps 25 000. It is unlikely that a single black rhino remains alive in the whole country.

That said, all is not lost and visitors can still be assured of seeing game, sometimes even in spectacular proportions, in game reserves that are among the most magnificent wildernesses on the continent. (Consult the chapters on regions for detailed descriptions of specific national parks and their game.)

Conservationists can take heart from the precedents set earlier in the century. If it is protected it will not take long for game in depleted reserves to return to its former numbers. The vital thing is that in Zambia, unlike so many African countries, the environment remains largely intact. Today the "parks" are run by the National Parks and Wildlife Service of Zambia (NPWS) which falls under the ministry of tourism. In addition to national parks, enormous areas around the parks and in places of environmental importance called Game Management Areas or GMAs have been declared. Together these areas amount to nearly 30 per cent of the whole country. (The map office in Lusaka publishes a map of these areas, which should be studied if you wish to fully understand conservation in Zambia.) In principle the GMAs act as buffer zones where people may live and controlled harvesting of natural resources is allowed. Some have plenty of game and in these safari hunters operate. A proportion of the money generated by hunting is then ploughed back into local communities under what is called the "Admade" programme. This is an attempt to give local populations a stake in conservation.

The infrastructure in Zambian national parks varies tremendously and their means of travel will determine which parks particular travellers will want to visit. Some can only be seen through specialised safari operators, while others have no infrastructure for visitors at all. Details and recommendations that may affect your choice are given in the regional chapters.

Permits are needed to enter national parks and the entry fees are expensive. These are arranged by safari companies if you visit the parks under their aegis, otherwise permits can be bought at park gates. Fees differ between the major parks and the more remote ones. At the moment the South Luangwa National Park costs US $15 per person per day. The Kafue, Lochinvar, Sumbu and Lower Zambezi cost $10 and the rest $5 per person per day. In addition vehicles are charged $10 per entry and camping in a national park costs $15 per adult per night. An angling permit can be bought for $10. For all remote parks it is recommended that permits be bought at Chilanga or regional NPWS offices. For further enquiries contact The Chief Warden, National Parks and Wildlife Service, Private Bag 1, Chilanga. A personal visit will prove far more effective. Drive south from Lusaka toward Kafue and Chirundu about 18 km and the head offices are located in bungalows on the left-hand side just as the road goes through a stand of tall eucalyptus trees.

General notes: Almost all national parks which visitors can tour in their own vehicles require four-wheel-drive vehicles. In some it is even wise to take two vehicles as a precaution against being stranded by mechanical failure very, very far from help.

When going into remote parks with no facilities it is recommended that you enquire at the nearest National Parks and Wildlife Service (NPWS) office for a guide. The local scouts have the only detailed knowledge of the areas and you will save yourself an enormous amount of frustrating thundering around in the bush by negotiating a scout's services for the duration of your visit. You will have to feed him, but he will bring his own bedding and – sometimes no small comfort – a rifle. In remote parks where there may still be poachers, one should consider that they are well armed and seldom friendly, although they are more likely to try and slip away unnoticed than provoke an encounter.

The lack of control in some parks places a great onus on visitors to be responsible. The wilderness is a precious thing, and in many ways its fate in Zambia lies in tourists' hands. Treat it as you would anything ancient and venerable – with the greatest respect. Where camping for example, although not yet formally required by law, it is environmentally friendly to remove and not simply bury all non-biodegradable waste.

Four-wheel-drive vehicles can wreck sensitive environments. Remember that game reserves were created to protect environments, not entertain tourists.

The bush requires common sense. In Zambia, where help will not always be at hand, it may save lives. Almost all wild animals can be dangerous. Avoid surprising animals who may think that attack is the best form of defence. Be very wary when walking along riverbanks; coming between hippos and water is a recipe for disaster. Don't even think about swimming. Be wary when drawing water. Crocodiles abound in even the most benign looking of Zambian waters. In any other encounter with dangerous game don't run, especially from lions. Remember they are cats and by comparison human beings are not very fleet-footed mice. Back off slowly, avoiding eye contact. In the unlikely event of being charged by any animal, you are more likely to survive if you stand your ground. The number of tourists who are eaten or trampled is on the increase. Again, the presence of an armed scout may be a comfort, if not a sensible precaution.

The national parks and important game areas are described in the following chapters on the regions within which they fall. A summary follows of location, why and how to go there, and what precautions are advised. For more information contact the National Parks and Wildlife Service, Private Bag 1, Chilanga; or the Zambian Wildlife Society, Box 30255, Lusaka, Tel. (01) 25-4226.

CANOEING AND RAFTING

Despite the attractions of many other rivers in Zambia, the Zambezi is the only river where canoeing and rafting are done commercially. Rafting is essentially restricted to the Victoria Falls where several companies on either side of the river vie for the privilege of offering you "the most exciting stretch of white water rafting in the world". For a more detailed description see chapter 7. Recently a company operating at the Sioma Falls has proposed rafting there (see chapter 8).

Canoeing is a more leisurely pursuit and several companies offer canoeing safaris either above the Victoria Falls (see chapter 7) or down the lower Zambezi (see chapter 6). A list of canoeing safari companies will be found in chapter 13. As opposed to the rafting, which is a hair-raising one-day affair, the canoe trips are spread across several days and the emphasis is on game- and birdwatching. Close encounters with big game on the shores and islands of the Zambezi during the silent passage of the canoes make this a unique way to see wildlife.

HIKING AND BACKPACKING

Alas, this is very underdeveloped in Zambia and suitable hiking environments are limited. Certain safari operators offer guided backpacking walking safaris in the Kafue and the Luangwa Valley national parks, which are the most exciting way of seeing big-game country (see chapters 6, 11 and 13). But there are no hiking trails that backpackers can follow on their own. At the moment the best on offer is the Nyika Plateau where you can walk for miles or take a guided hike of several days, but that is essentially a Malawi experience.

BIRDWATCHING

Many parts of Zambia remain sparsely populated areas of pristine wilderness and therefore excellent locations for birdwatching. Diverse habitats from Kalahari sandveld to lakes and forests host numerous species found nowhere else.

There are a number of books available for identification although the specific field guide to the birds of Zambia is out of print. Southern African guides like Roberts or Newman's *Birds of Southern Africa* combined with Newman's *Birds of Malawi* and a guide to the birds of East and Central Africa cover most species.

Good birding areas

The Kafue Flats

Possibly the best-known locations for birdwatching in the country are the floodplains of the Blue Lagoon and Lochinvar national parks, north and south respectively of the Kafue River. A huge variety of local and migratory birds are to be found – over 430 species have been recorded. Local fig trees may conceal the rare and endemic Chaplin's Barbet. Standing near the water's edge and watching clouds of pratincoles and waterfowl drift and sway across the azure landscape is a magnificent experience.

The Zambezi below Victoria Falls

The river between the falls and the lower Zambezi Valley covers a wide range of habitat especially good for thicket and riparian forest birds. Kariba itself is rather disappointing, although it hosts a vast number of fish eagles. The Zambezi marks the southern limit of many central African species and so well defined is the valley barrier that many species found on the Zambian side do not occur in Zimbabwe. These include Fullerborn's longclaw, pale-billed hornbills, the miombo pied barbet, the central bearded scrub robin, Bohm's flycatcher and the white-tailed blue flycatcher. Unfortunately the damming of Kariba destroyed the flood cycle on which some species, such as the African skimmers and rock pratincoles, depended for breeding.

The Zambezi Valley hosts a huge variety of birds of prey and the Batoka Gorge is a particularly remarkable area for nesting raptors. Although the gorge is difficult to access the avid birdwatcher will be rewarded by the possibility of some 36 species, including the rare taita falcon, bat hawks, peregrine falcons, ospreys, black and crowned eagles and western banded snake eagles.

Below the Kariba wall the roads to Chirundu, Mbendele and Mutulanganga pass through very good bird areas with the hot summer months producing such special finds as Narina trogons, barred cuckoos, Livingstone's flycatcher, white spotted nicator and the mottled and batlike spinetails. And perhaps most prized of all the beautiful Angola pitta can be found in surrounding thickets.

The Upper Zambezi, the Kafue National Park and the Busanga floodplains

Habitats in this region are large and varied, from floodplain and grassland to riparian woodland, "miombo" woodland, Kalahari sandveld and mopane forest.

Special birds include Chaplin's barbets, a Zambian endemic found in fig savanna, black-cheeked lovebirds (which are a Red Data species) and Pel's fishing owl in the riverine woodlands. Denham's bustard can be found west of the Zambezi. The Busanga plains host huge flocks of wattled cranes, pelicans and pratincoles as well as Bohm's bee-eaters and African skimmers. Carmine bee-eaters nest in magnificent colonies along the main rivers.

Mwinilunga and the north-west

High rainfall in this area produces equatorial forest and well developed riparian forest which together with large grassy "dambos" and pans make for excellent birding. Many rare and interesting birds are to be found here, including white-spotted flufftails, olive long-tailed cuckoos, Grimwood's longclaw and thrush babblers. The West Lunga National Park is a particularly good area for such species although the park itself is difficult to access.

The Nyika Plateau and north eastern montane forests

Visitors to this area should be equipped with Newman's *Birds of Malawi* and be on the lookout for Angolan and red-rumped swallows, pink-breasted turtle doves, bartailed trogons, Sharpe's akalat and scarlet-tufted malachite sunbirds. The habitat is quite unique and so has many species not found anywhere else in Zambia. In order to spot the birds one is advised to walk very slowly and quietly or simply sit and wait in likely areas as forest birds feed "on the hop", as it were, are wary and often feed in travelling bird parties.

The Bangweulu Swamps

This area is unfortunately most difficult to access during the best birding season after the rains but a visit at any time of year is worthwhile, with most wetland species being found here. It is particularly well known as the most southerly locale of that extraordinary bird, the shoebill. On Shoebill Island they can be seen at particularly close quarters. Other species include coppery-tailed coucals, white-rumped barbets and marsh tchagras, endemic to northern Zambia. Long-toed flufftails can be found in open dambos.

Northern Zambia and the Great Lakes

Population density in much of northern Zambia has resulted in habitat degradation in some areas. However, many species can still be found that do not occur further south. Shoebills occur in several marshes. Lake Mweru has some interesting localised species such as the Payn's yellow warbler, slender-billed weaver, orange-cheeked waxbill and spotted thrush-babbler. Red and blue sunbirds are beautiful birds found over much of northern Zambia and a very localised monotypic genus of white-winged starling occurs only in the upper Luangwa and on Lake Mweru Wantipa. The spectacular Lady Ross's tauraco, more dowdily known as Ross's loerie, is common in the northern provinces. Palm nut vultures can be found in the phoenix palms along the tributaries of the Chambeshi. The Kapishya hot springs near Shiwa Ngandu are a particularly good location for these last two species.

The Luangwa Valley

This extensive and pristine wilderness is a prime location for both game- and birdwatching. Most of the species found here are similar to those in the Zambezi Valley, but they have been more extensively recorded, particularly in the region around Mfuwe. A local speciality is Pel's fishing owl. There are large numbers of African skimmers along the sandbanks of the Luangwa. In the miombo woodlands the elusive African broadbill can be seen doing its delightful aerial display and the bar-winged weaver, a miombo endemic, may be found.

Zambia has a small but very active ornithological society, ZOS, from whom more extensive information on the country's birdlife can be obtained. ZOS has an annual subscription of £20 or US $30. Their address is Box 33944, Lusaka. For philatelists Zambia has produced a collection of exquisitely painted stamps of special Zambian birds.

ANGLING

Zambia is estimated to have 45 per cent of the total water resources of southern Africa. So it's little wonder that the multitude of rivers, lakes and swamps host an enormous and varied fish population. Obviously only a fraction of these will interest anglers, but many species that occur here are not found elsewhere in southern Africa. Despite its enormous potential, sport fishing is relatively underdeveloped in Zambia, so it presents keen anglers with all sorts of exciting possibilities.

The premier fishing destinations are the Zambezi and Kafue rivers, Lake Kariba and Lake Tanganyika, but that should not deter keen sportsmen from trying other areas. Angling is even allowed in national parks as long as a permit has been obtained beforehand.

For the most part the hot summer months are the best fishing season except in the Barotse floodplains of the upper Zambezi where June through to August are said to be best. Anglers are advised to take their own equipment and paraphernalia as there are no stores selling tackle anywhere in the country. Boats are only available at some lodges. Remember that very strict regulations control the movement of boats between the waters of different countries in southern Africa. Fishing from banks is often difficult and even dangerous with few waters free of crocodiles and some positively infested with the reptiles.

Some of the better known destinations, their angling possibilities and where necessary particular fishing techniques are described here.

The Zambezi and its tributaries

One of the longest rivers in the world with diverse habitats as well as huge waterfalls and rapids that form obstacles to the passage of different species, the Zambezi naturally has a wealth of fishing opportunities. The river is probably most famous for tigerfish. These are caught on a variety of spinners, spoons or baits and methods vary from place to place. There are numerous bream species including yellow-bellied, three-spot, redbreasted, Kariba and Mozambique breams. Then there are a host of others worth catching, some with quite ludicrous names such as vundu, thin-faced largemouth, pink happy, green happy, cheesa, nkupi, bottlenose and Cornish jack.

Angling destinations may be divided into those above and below the Victoria Falls, and between Lake Kariba, the lower Zambezi and the Kafue River. The upper Zambezi and Barotse floodplains (see chapters 7 and 8) are an excellent destination in the dry season when the flood-waters recede from the surrounding floodplains, concentrating food sources on the river. Popular fishing spots are Senanga, Mongu and the Sioma Falls and Sesheke or Katima Mulilo. There are a limited number of professional angling safari operations. Barotse Fishing Safaris operate out of Senanga. The Senanga Lodge has a few boats and some equipment for hire. Tiger Fishing Tours Ltd have a tented camp about 35 km north of Mongu. Below the Ngonye Falls at Sioma where the Zambezi narrows, fishing from the banks is said to be good. About 20 km downstream from the falls there is a small rustic camp located about 2 km south of where the powerlines cross the river. Further downstream there are no operators or places to stay until the vicinity of Livingstone. These lodges and safari companies are described in chapters 12 and 13.

Lake Kariba itself is an angling haven. It is un-commercialised on the Zambian side and indeed only really accessible at Sinazongwe and Siavonga. Some lodges at Siavonga provide boats. The best time to fish at Kariba is between October and March. The lower Zambezi is a fine fishing location although of the few camps on this stretch of the river (see chapter 6), most are closed during the wet season when fishing is at its best.

The Kafue River presents an anomaly to anglers because certain species such as the tigerfish, which are present in all the other tributaries of the Zambezi, are not found above the Kafue Gorge. This is explained by the Kafue Gorge rapids and a fascinating theory which indicates that the upper and lower Zambezi were once different rivers altogether. For more details see Mike Main's book *Zambezi, Journey of a River*. The Kafue is famous for its yellow-bellied bream which are caught along its entire length. Lafupa and Chunga camps in the Kafue National Park have motorised launches. There is Lechwe Lodge not far from Lusaka and Gwabi Lodge very close to where the Kafue joins the Zambezi near Chirundu.

Lake Tanganyika

This enormous lake (see chapter 10) has so many fish species that many have not even been named yet. But there are several well known to anglers which make this a premier destination. There are kupi, salmon, Goliath tigerfish and the redoubtable Nile perch, for which these are the most southern waters. The lake is very clear and extremely deep with an obstruction-free bottom. This has led to a curious type of angling in which special enlarged "lips" are added to deep diving lures, then trolled on thin (2-4 kg) line up to 200 m behind the boat. A downrigger would probably work just as well.

The kupi is probably the most sought-after fish. Swallow-tailed and gold in colour, it can weigh 4 kg and is usually caught on small deep diving lures or fillet baits fished near the bottom. Once hooked it is a tenacious fighter and once cooked quite the most delicious fish from the lake.

This Rift Valley lake is renowned for its Nile perch, although this species does not attain the gargantuan proportions of its Lake Victoria relative. But specimens up to 50 kg are landed, often while fishing for nkupi with artificial deep diving lures at depths over 30 m. They are not especially good fighters but their slightly oily flesh can be good eating.

Perhaps the most exciting fish to hook in the lake is the Goliath tigerfish, which is much larger, more fearsome and every bit as good a fighter as its smaller southern cousin. This monster really belongs to the Zaïre River drainage system but can be found here in the estuaries of major rivers entering the lake. Generally the Zambian shores are not the best areas on the lake for fishing, because they are shallower than others but in February each year the Zambian National Angling Championship is contested out of Kasaba Bay. For more details about the tournament write to Regg Hueys at Box 90669, Luanshya. He has organised the tournament ever since its inception over 20 years ago.

Although sport angling is only beginning to realise its potential in Zambia, the local population have of course been fishing the waters for years. Unregulated use of gill nets and the like has depleted resources on some rivers, especially in heavily populated areas. Despite this, the fishing remains excellent and angling locations are often as wild and pristine as one could wish for. For visitors particularly interested in fish and fishing, Paul Skelton's *A Complete Guide to the Freshwater Fishes of Southern Africa* (Southern Books 1993) is highly recommended.

HUNTING SAFARIS

Zambia is renowned for offering some of the finest big-game hunting in Africa. Game management areas have been described earlier, and it is in these vast wildernesses surrounding and unfenced from the major national parks that safari hunting takes place. Swamps and savanna, deciduous woodland, Kalahari sandveld, forests and plains provide habitats for a diverse game population, with several species endemic to Zambia. Heavy poaching in the last decade has considerably reduced game populations. In an effort to reverse this tendency the government has introduced a system called the Administrative Management Design or Admade policy for Zambia's game management areas. The principle underlying Admade is that local residents will derive financial benefit from hunting and thereby be motivated to care for and to manage their environments with the help of the National Parks and Wildlife Service. Ideally game will thus be protected and returns accruing to local communities can be used to upgrade their services and facilities.

The hunting coincides with the dry season between May and October/November. Temperatures are quite low through to September when they start rising rapidly. Hunting in the Luangwa in October can be a hot business indeed. During these months hunters in Zambia can hunt three of the "big five", namely lion, buffalo and leopard. There is a moratorium on shooting elephants and there are no rhino left at all. In addition Zambian "specialities" include sitatunga, red lechwe, Lichtenstein's hartebeest, sable and roan and the endemic species of black lechwe, Kafue lechwe, Cooksons's wildebeest and Defassa waterbuck. The chosen prey will determine the area of the country you are likely to hunt in and the appropriate safari company.

All hunters are required to purchase hunting licences and further to abide by the rules and regulations laid down by the NPWS. There are a number of regulations regarding hunting with hand guns or bows and arrows. Temporary importation of firearms and ammunition is possible, as is the export of trophies, but all sorts of regulations must be observed and before coming to the country to hunt you are advised to contact the Professional Hunters Association of Zambia at Box 30106, Lusaka, or telephone them on Lusaka 21-1644, Fax 22-6736 or Telex ZA44460. A list of professional hunters and safari companies will also be provided by the association.

FESTIVALS AND CULTURAL EVENTS

Not surprisingly in a country with such a diverse cultural heritage many Zambian tribes have special events or festivals that celebrate their particular culture. Most of these are well worth seeing if your trip coincides with them and the very grandest, such as the *Kuomboka*, are worth a trip to see in their own right. Major tourist centres such as Livingstone and some of the biggest hotels have displays of traditional dancing, but these are a poor imitation of the real thing.

The *Kuomboka* ceremony of Barotseland is perhaps the most remarkable and exciting traditional ceremony left in Africa. The name means "to get out of the water onto dry ground". The heart of Barotseland is the vast Barotse floodplain that lies either side of the Zambezi River. The Lozi, a proud and beautiful people, live on the plain. Lozi traditions and agrarian culture are tied to the annual flood cycle of the river. Barotseland is no longer the independent kingdom it once was but the Lozi remain loyal to their traditional ruler, the Lozi King or "Litunga". The present Litunga is king Yeta IV. He is the representative of Western Province in government.

At the end of the annual rainy season the Zambezi overflows its banks in Barotseland and the surrounding grasslands are suddenly turned into a vast and shimmering lake of green and azure. As the waters begin to rise, usually in April, the Lozi people (and an increasing number of other Zambians and world media) wait in excited anticipation. Then at a time of his choosing, preferably on a Thursday immediately prior to the full moon, and not in the least affected by all the outside attention, the Litunga beats the royal war drums to signal his readiness to move from the lowland palace at Lealui to his high ground residence at Limulunga. Three huge drums named the Kanaona, Munanga and Mundili, each said to be over 170 years old, are brought into the royal courtyard. These drums are over a metre wide and deep and resonate far over Barotseland telling everyone that the king will not sleep at Lealui that night and summoning his subjects to the *Kuomboka* ceremony. Once the king has started the drumming, the royal drummers will keep up the beat continuously until they are taken onto the Litunga's barge, the *Nalikwanda*.

The *Nalikwanda*, depicted in paintings and tourist magazines across the country, is an enormous wooden canoe built by a German carpenter at the beginning of the century and painted with broad black and white stripes. A large half-dome of reeds and canvas protects the king from the sun. Surmounted on top is a big black paper mache elephant and above it flies the Litunga's flag, brilliant red with the silhouette of an elephant.

Enthroned on the barge, the Litunga is powered from Lealui to Limulunga by over 100 paddlers. It is a great honour to be a paddler. Each paddler wears a knee-length skirt draped with various animal skins and a scarlet beret or turban topped by a tuft of lion's mane hair as a headdress. They row with great vigour, but if the *Macabula* drum is sounded, it signals that one paddler is not exerting himself enough and the unfortunate is immediately and unceremoniously thrown overboard by the other paddlers. Throughout the day-long journey the royal orchestra of xylophones and drums proclaim the passage of the king. Following behind in a slightly smaller but equally resplendent barge, the *Nalola*, comes the queen and behind her a flotilla of attendants, dignitaries and onlookers. Three white-painted dugouts scout ahead for suitable channels for the *Nalikwanda* and the procession to follow. At the end of the day the royal harbour, Nyayuma, at Limulunga is reached and the king is enticed ashore by women dancing in traditional dress.

When the king steps forth from the *Nalikwanda* he is no longer dressed traditionally but splendidly attired in the full uniform of a British admiral, complete with gold braided jacket and ostrich plumed hat, all tailor-made in London at the time of his ascendancy to the Lozi throne. As he steps ashore his subjects chant and give the royal salute or *kushowelela* by kneeling, raising their hands above their heads and then bowing until their foreheads touch the ground. The ceremony ends when the king is taken into the winter capital and all Barotseland succumbs to a night of feasting and celebration with many a reveller passing the remainder of the day, if not the week, in a state of somewhat impaired vision.

During the ceremony, accommodation in nearby Mongu or even Senanga is all but impossible to find. Most hotels in Mongu hold special *Kuomboka* functions. One should try to book early although this is made rather difficult by the unpredictability of the event. The Zambian National Tourist Board attempts to give the earliest possible confirmation of the date.

Sounding rather similar, but in fact quite different is the *Umutomboko*, which is a colourful ceremony in Luapula Province. In a specially prepared arena on the banks of the Ng'ona River, Senior Chief Kazembe celebrates the heritage of one of the great old central African empires by dancing the ancestral war dance, the *Mutomboko*. It takes place on the nearest weekend to the end of July.

The *Likumbi lya Mize* is held by the Luvale people of north-western Zambia when they come together to display their traditional crafts – a process accompanied by much traditional dancing and singing. It takes place every July at Mize, some 7 km west of the town of Zambezi, where the senior Luvale chief, Chief Ndungu, has his palace.

Shimunenga is a tradition of the Ila or Ba-Ila of southern Zambia. It is a ceremony of devotion to the divine ancestors of the tribe and it is usually celebrated either in September or October on a weekend closest to the full moon at Maala, which is on the Kafue Flats about 35 km west of Namwala.

The Ngoni of eastern Zambia have a religious ceremony of thanksgiving for the harvest in which Chief Mpenzi samples the first fruits of the harvest. It takes place at Mutenguleni village near Chipata on February 24. Like most traditional ceremonies this is accompanied by the consumption of vast quantities of beer and lots of dancing, and Ngoni dancing is something of a local speciality. The traditional *Vimbuza* dancer, bedecked in vivid, gaudy colours dances for many special occasions. Then there are the masked dancers, the *Nyau*, who are rather more difficult for the public to see, being associated with tribal cults and rituals.

BUYING CRAFTS AND SOUVENIRS

Crafts and curios are not as readily available in Zambia as for example in Zimbabwe, where vast quantities are flogged along the roadside. There are craft shops in the major centres, the biggest hotels and at Lusaka Airport. But generally the quality of goods is dubious and the shops are full of kitsch curios and trinkets that could have been made anywhere.

In Lusaka, Bush Crafts on Cairo Road, just across Church Road from the post office, is an exception. It has a range of really authentic traditional items at reasonable prices. Other shops include the Wildlife Shop next door and Busanga Arts and Crafts, also on Cairo Road, and the Kabwata Cultural Centre.

In Livingstone some vendors flog carvings just off the main road near the Tourist Information offices. Rather better quality wood carving is to be found in the craft shop next to the Falls themselves.

An essential stop for curio buyers who are going that way is the Tonga Craft Museum in Choma, which not only exhibits some of the finest authentic crafts from all over Zambia but has a shop selling articles of excellent quality.

Crafts in the Copperbelt seem restricted to articles carved in malachite which are certainly not to everybody's taste.

Along the road to Siavonga villagers will rush out with enormous hunks of amethyst and other semi-precious stones. People buying jewellery would do well to be cautious of the young men vending precious stones and articles made from them at petrol stations and other outlets. Most of these offerings are complete junk. It is possible that genuine precious stones and diamonds are brought to Zambia from Zaïre and Angola, but this trade is illegal, and besides you have to be quite an expert to determine whether the pieces are authentic.

By far the best way to find genuine crafts is to buy them from rural villages, where you can be sure the articles are authentic and your money goes directly to the craftsman or owner. Beautiful reed and papyrus mats are made in Western Province. Here you will see people walking along with genuine spears and bows and arrows, and good furniture is made in the region too. The Lunda in North-western Province make masks as well as extraordinary arrowheads with symbolic and ritualistic significance. Basketware seems better in eastern Zambia. Different kinds of fishing baskets and traps are made all over the country and every village has a couple of old maize stampers.

Remember that in Zimbabwe the tourist preference for huge rough wooden carvings poses a serious environmental threat and it would be as well not to encourage the trend in Zambia.

PHOTOGRAPHY

The writer Shiva Naipaul wrote of his brief visit to Zambia in his otherwise riveting book *North of South*:

"The Zambian landscape is one note endlessly repeated . . . unending woodland, a featureless wilderness of spindly trees . . . [that] for mile after mile, hour after hour remains the same."

To some extent that is true of many stretches of road in Zambia, but whether the landscape will provoke such boredom in most visitors is another question. Certainly Naipaul spared little imagination to find the beauty in such enormous tracts of unspoiled environment and had no time to see the many splendid variations on the theme; from the spectacular vastness of the western plains, the ineffable might of the Zambezi, Kafue and Luapula rivers, from green rushes shuddering with life on lake and swamp shore to the endless azure of their horizons, from sombre forests and mesmerising waterfalls to the riotous laissez-faire of contemporary Zambian towns.

Except in the South Luangwa wildlife is shy from years of poaching, but such diffidence is sometimes made up for by sheer numbers. However telephotos are essential, with 200 mm lenses being the minimum size necessary. It is a case of the bigger the better. Because stability becomes a problem with big lenses, take a bean cushion, drape it over the window and support the camera on it – raising or lowering the window as desired. If you will be in an open vehicle take a tripod, but unless you are in a private party these can be cumbersome on game drives. It is not the sort of country where you will get great game shots on foot. Zambia has wide, wide horizons for which a wide angle is indispensable. Most people in Zambia will not object to having their photograph taken. But a few, particularly old rural women, object on superstitious grounds and an increasing number feel they are being exploited by photographers. Always ask. Some subjects will demand money but they can usually be won over with a few minutes of idle banter. Markets are always a source of life and colour. Cultural events such as the *Kuomboka* ceremony particularly lend themselves to photography. Snotty and trachoma-riddled children will swarm around you and young men are quite happy to waste your entire film on a series of the most forced and outlandish poses.

In contrast to Naipaul's disenchantment, the authors' experience is that no amount of camera film is enough. Estimate what you think you will need and double it. Take everything with you, especially spare batteries – which are extremely difficult to find even in the main centres. Video enthusiasts should have an ample supply of charged batteries because opportunities to recharge them will be few and far between. Many lodges and camps do not have electricity and many hotel rooms do not have usable plugs. Do pack your equipment in robust, well cushioned and dustproof bags or cases. Things get bashed around on Zambian roads and dust seeps into everything, so take lens cleaning cloths and brushes. Remember to take a waterproof bag for photographing the Victoria Falls.

Daylight is usually harsh, so early mornings and evenings are best. Film ratings of 50 or 100 ASA are recommended.

African skin is surprisingly difficult to photograph so use a fill-in flash for people shots to avoid high contrast. For wide-angle scenic shots a polarising filter is definitely recommended to bring out depth and reduce glare.

6 THE CENTRAL REGION

The central region, being the hub of the country, is well developed and densely populated as one would expect. Zambia's most important roads radiate from Lusaka and particularly around the city they can be heavily congested. But it is quite remarkable how quickly the populated peri-urban area can be left behind. The great wilderness of the lower Zambezi Valley falls away practically from Lusaka's eastern suburbs; the wild Lunsemfwa River valley is barely 100 km away as the crow flies; Blue Lagoon in the Kafue Flats is a similar distance to the west and the Kafue National Park, one of the biggest game reserves in the world, is only four hours away by road. The people of the central region embrace several of Zambia's tribes and languages. The predominant language is probably Nyanja in the city and eastwards, but westwards to the Kafue most people probably speak Kaonde.

LUSAKA

The capital of Zambia will probably be most airborne visitors' first contact with the country and an unavoidable interlude for anyone else on a comprehensive tour. Generally disliked by visitors and residents alike, it's a bustling, energetic city perhaps too gripped by a mercantile and bureaucratic fervour to have ever taken much care of its appearance. Yet it is not without a certain shambolic charm and its people are friendly and cosmopolitan.

The name Lusaka is derived from that of a Lenje headman, Lusaaka, whose village lay nearby at the coming of the railway and the building of a siding in 1906. Otherwise relatively uninhabited the area was notorious for lions, and indeed the very night that the siding was laid lions killed several oxen almost beneath the wheels of the shunting engine. Catholic missionaries followed the railway, and then white settlers in the form of Boer families displaced by the Anglo-Boer War in South Africa. The first humble precursor of today's monolithic tower blocks was a wattle and daub store built in 1908. Thereafter expansion followed rapidly and the town was gazetted in 1913, but when the First World War broke out building stopped and between 1915 and 1929 the town stagnated.

Built on limestone, Lusaka had no surface water supply during the dry season but was annually flooded during the rains. Despite such inadequacies its central location persuaded the colonial administration in 1930 to move the capital here from Livingstone, and a minor building boom began on the higher ground to the east of the railway line and Cairo Road. Government House (now State House) and the British South Africa Company offices (now the Ministry of Foreign Affairs) were built in a Georgian style. The area became known as "snobs' hill" and in 1933 the governor commented: "It is . . . quite apparent . . . that there are the most hideous buildings growing up all over Lusaka." In 1935 it was officially proclaimed the capital of Northern Rhodesia. After the Second World War thousands of new settlers arrived in the country and development spread to create the vast incoherent sprawl of mixed suburbia, business and administration that the city is today.

Incredibly, by 1960 Lusaka still did not have a waterborne sewerage system and relied solely on night soil wagons. Cairo Road was described by a visiting British peer as "surely the greatest spectacle since the Calgary stampede . . ." His reservations did not deter the Queen, who in 1955 conferred by royal charter upon Lusaka the "style and dignity of a city".

Independence in 1964 provoked the obvious rush of name changes and another building boom. Before the economy collapsed several new tower blocks were built along Cairo Road, rather throwing "style and dignity" to the winds with monumental scale taking priority over beauty and imagination.

Today a thoroughly modern skyline rears up to proclaim the city's metropolitan stature over the surrounding bush.

Access

By air: Zambia's main international airport is located just outside Lusaka on the Great East Road. There are car hire companies at the airport; the Pamodzi and Intercontinental hotels have courtesy buses and there are plenty of taxis in which a ride into the city will cost about US $15. Zambian taxis do not have meters, so be sure to establish the fare beforehand. Generally fares seem to be controlled by some unwritten code, but you may be able to knock them down a few per cent by haggling. From the airport the Great East Road brings one straight into town via the University of Zambia and the agricultural showgrounds. Proceed straight for the CBD, meeting Cairo Road at its north end circle or turn left after the showgrounds up Addis Ababa Drive to the administrative and embassy belt and the chief hotels. The Pamodzi Hotel is on the right just before Church Road; the Ridgeway Hotel is on the corner of Church Road and Independence Avenue; and the Intercontinental on Haile Selassie Avenue, 100 m beyond the circle in front of the supreme court.

By rail: Rail passengers will arrive from either north or south at the main station just east of Cairo Road. The closest hotel is the Lusaka Hotel, directly opposite on the corner of Katondo and Cairo roads.

By bus: The intercity bus terminal is close to the station, to the east of and opposite the railway line from Cairo Road. UBZ, the national carrier, has several buses daily coming to Lusaka from all corners of the country.

By car: Travellers coming in their own vehicles will arrive in Lusaka one of four ways. They may come from the south on the Kafue Road, which runs straight into Cairo Road at its south end circle; from the north at its opposite end; down the Great East Road past the airport as described above, or from the west on the Mumbwa Road. This route, perhaps the most confusing of the four, passes through the chaotic commercial belt and ultimately joins Cairo Road about halfway along its length.

Tourist information

Most travel agencies, airline offices and car hire offices are located on Cairo Road. For general information the Zambian National Tourist Board has offices in Century House, opposite Kingstons bookshop on Lusaka Square, Cairo Road.

Lusaka can be divided into areas west and east of the railway line. The CBD lies on a narrow grid along Cairo Road, but the greater metropolitan area of Lusaka lies to the east of Cairo Road on the other side of the railway line. It is a confusing sprawl of boulevards, tree-lined avenues and a spidery web of suburban roads laid out according to some unique and incomprehensible logic of its own. Visitors planning to stay in Lusaka for any length of time would do well to buy a map of the city, available from the Zambia National Tourist Board office, the map office in the Department of Survey, Mulungushi House, Bushcrafts curio shop or possibly from the gift shops of the big hotels.

Lusaka is known for its petty crime, but if you keep your wits about you it is, like the rest of the country, quite safe. Violent crime is most

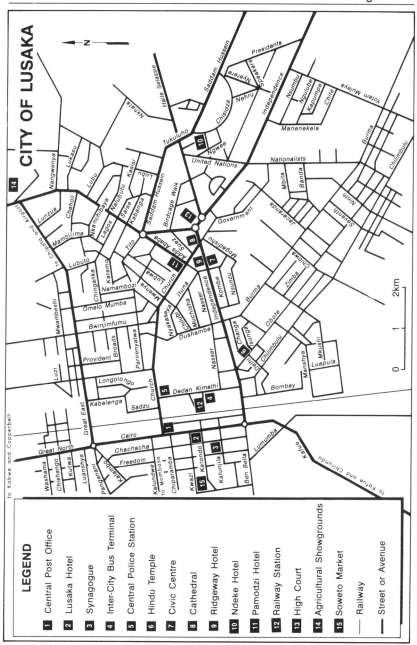

CITY OF LUSAKA

LEGEND

1 Central Post Office
2 Lusaka Hotel
3 Synagogue
4 Inter-City Bus Terminal
5 Central Police Station
6 Hindu Temple
7 Civic Centre
8 Cathedral
9 Ridgeway Hotel
10 Ndeke Hotel
11 Pamodzi Hotel
12 Railway Station
13 High Court
14 Agricultural Showgrounds
15 Soweto Market
— Railway
— Street or Avenue

unlikely but you flaunt expensive cameras and the like at your own risk and drivers of new-looking motor cars should leave someone to watch the vehicle if they park.

Cairo Road: Really a junction on the Great North Road, the name captures the sense of history and vision that the facades of its blighted buildings have lost. First-time visitors are likely to be rather dismayed by the chaotic stream of traffic that surges up one side of the avenue and washes back down the other at peak hours. If walking on the thronging pavements makes you insecure, the tree avenue in the middle offers more elbow room. In October the trees burst into flower, temporarily garlanding the shabby street in brilliant scarlet bloom. If the paving slabs beneath the trees have a slightly hollow sound it's because beneath them still lies the cesspit that originally ran down the middle of the road. At night the street changes abruptly and becomes deserted and dark. Walking around at night is obviously more dangerous.

Cairo Road is the hub of the retail sector. Although window dressing is limited, most basic shopping requirements will be met and there are several supermarkets that offer a wide range of foodstuffs and beverages. For curios try Bushcrafts and the Wildlife shop across Church Road from the main post office. The Wildlife shop also sells maps and information booklets about Lusaka and the rest of the country.

Almost all the main banks as well as several bureaus de change can be found on Cairo Road. Deregulation of currency exchange will probably lead to the demise of the bureaus in time, and it will be possible to change money over the counter at any bank.

The area west of Cairo Road is mostly commercial and light industrial. The motor industries particularly are to be found here. The public library and information centre lies just behind the Lusaka Hotel. It is a well-known place for black market money changing, but be careful because it is a less than salubrious area.

The "Soweto" market lies a few blocks west of Cairo Road, between Nkwazi and Katondo roads. It really defies any description beyond that implied in the name, but in its shanty-lined alleyways can be found almost anything you would care to buy if you're not concerned about its origins. It is particularly good for vehicle spare parts. What cannot be found can be "ordered" and usually produced within a day, no questions asked. Do be very careful about prices though; while Zambians will not engage in protracted bargaining as is the practice in some countries, initial prices are always high and cheaper deals are only arrived at by making a reasonable counter-offer.

Only three roads connect the CBD on Cairo Road with the government sector and embassy belt of the eastern suburbs on the other side of the railway line. The Great East Road runs from the north end circle, Church Road is next to the post office midway along Cairo Road, and Independence Avenue runs from the south end circle. Of these Independence Avenue gives most direct access to the government buildings, embassies, hotels and suburbs. Cathedral Hill is the centre of this area, but the name is something of a misnomer, as it is only marginally higher than the rest of the city. It is composed mostly of a huge traffic circle with the new Anglican Cathedral at one end, the supreme court opposite the intersection of Independence Avenue and the secretariat at the other end. Don't try to photograph government buildings – for all the openness under the new government Zambians still get uptight about security.

Accommodation

Lusaka has a range of hotels and places to stay, none of them particularly cheap. The main city hotels are located in the suburbs a few kilometres east of the CBD. The Pamodzi is the most luxurious and most expensive. Then on a sliding scale there is the Holiday Inn Ridgeway on the corner of Church Road and Independence Avenue and the Intercontinental on Haile Selassie Avenue. Slightly more downmarket, but in some ways more charming is the Ndeke Hotel on the corner of Haile Selassie Avenue and Saddam Hussein Boulevard. The only hotel right in the CBD is the Lusaka Hotel, the oldest hotel in the city, but it is rather claustrophobic although reasonably priced. There are several other options a few kilometres out of town, of which the most exclusive is Lilayi Lodge. It is located on a game farm off the Kafue Road, so provides tremendous relief from the bustle of the city. There is the Hillview, which is small and quiet, and Andrews Motel which is rather the opposite. On the Great East Road between the city and the airport there are the Chainama and Barn motels and on the Mumbwa Road there is the Garden House Hotel. The best alternative for campers is a new facility called Eureka. It is well signposted on the left-hand side as one heads south from the city on the Kafue Road.

See chapter 13 for more details. Remember that foreign visitors are required to settle their bills in foreign currency in almost all hotels. If you are spending several days in town it is worth asking your hotel for special rates which may offer as much as a 20 per cent discount.

Places of interest in Lusaka

Tours of the city can be arranged through the major travel agencies. Lusaka isn't brimming with exciting sights for tourists. Apart from absorbing the hubbub on Cairo Road, adventurous visitors might enjoy the two markets, of which the most prominent is visible from the Independence Avenue bridge. Nowadays it's a venue for "Salaula" – Zambia's controversial second-hand clothing trade – but colourful cloth and reed mats can also be found. The other is the Soweto market described above. If at your wit's end for something to do, try the following.

The Lusaka Museum and Mulungushi Convention Centre. The museum is in the centre and it is really just an exposition of Zambia's political history. The centre itself was built by Kenneth Kaunda to host a summit of the so-called non-aligned states in 1970. The centre is located just off the Great East Road about 1,5 km east of the intersection with Addis Ababa Drive.

The National Archives. Government Road. Open during regular government hours. There's an African Library and photo exhibits. Maps may be for sale.

The National Assembly. Nanquenya Road (off Addis Ababa Drive). Tours of this, the Zambian parliament building, are conducted on the last Thursday of the month.

Civic Centre. Independence Avenue. Contains Lusaka's municipal offices. The adjoining Nakatindi Hall is used for big official functions.

The Cultural Village at Kabwata. Burma Road. On-site craftsmen produce curios in wood and malachite. There used to be cultural dancing, but this seems to have fallen away.

The Moore Pottery Factory in Kabelenga Road is easily accessed from Cairo Road. Take Church Road over the bridge then turn second left; it's about a kilometre down on the right.

The Munda Wanga Botanical Gardens are 16 km down the Kafue Road and although the zoo is dismal the gardens are worth a visit. There are swimming pools and picnic areas.

The University of Zambia is set in very attractive grounds off the Great East Road. It is a modern campus and has some of Zambia's better modern architecture.

Picnic places

Munda Wanga, described above.

Chongwe River, 42 km further down the Great East Road from the university.

The Kafue Marina is located on the Kafue River about 50 km from Lusaka. Turn left just before the bridge. Boats may be hired.

Restaurants

Lusaka boasts neither a great number nor selection of restaurants. In addition to the main hotels, the following are popular.

El Toro Restaurant, 725 Freedom Way, to the west of Cairo Road.

The Lotus Inn is on Cairo Road.

Nsaku Chinese Restaurant. Next to the Tourist Board in Century House, Lusaka Square.

Gringo's Grill Restaurant. 2229 Lubu Road. Tel: 25-3337.

Marco Polo at the Polo Club. Agricultural showgrounds. Tel: 2-5011.

Golden Spoon Lusaka (Holiday Inn Garden Court) Tel: 25–4571.

Nightclubs

If nightclubbing takes your fancy you could try either the Moon City night club or Valentino's, which are both located in Indeco House on Buteko Place off Cairo Road. The only place recommended to the authors was called, rather bizarrely, Mike's Car Wash – situated on the right-hand side of the Kafue Road as you head south out of town. Apparently it is the place to see and hear local bands.

Sporting facilities

Sports facilities for tourists in Lusaka are fairly limited. The Lusaka municipal sports club and Lusaka central sports club are located just off Alick Nkata Avenue.

There are three golf courses in and around Lusaka. Most central is the Lusaka golf course, which is on Saddam Hussein Boulevard, Tel: 25-1598/25-0244/25-0831. The Chainama Hills golf course is on Kalingalinga Road, Tel: 25-1010/29-1300. The Chilanga club is clearly signposted off the Kafue Road at Chilanga, Tel: 27-8417/27-8323. Non-members are usually charged a fee of US $10 to play at these clubs.

The Intercontinental has tennis courts which can be hired for about 1 000 kwacha. Both the Intercontinental and the Pamodzi have squash courts and several hotels have swimming pools. In addition the Pamodzi Hotel has a fully equipped gymnasium, available to non-guests at a membership fee of US $400 a year!

Polo is a popular sport in Zambia, particularly among expatriates, and there are often matches on weekends at the Polo Club in the Lusaka showgrounds.

Soccer is far and away Zambia's most popular sport. Watch the press for details of matches in and around the city.

Places of worship

The Anglican Cathedral of the Holy Cross is on the corner of Independence Avenue and Chikwa Road.

Northmead Assembly of God is located at the Northmead shopping centre off the Great East Road.

There is a Baptist Church in Lubu Road, between Addis Ababa Drive and Saddam Hussein Boulevard.

St Ignatius Catholic Church is located on Addis Ababa Drive near the showgrounds.

The Presbyterian Church of St Columbus is on Addis Ababa Drive.

There is a Seventh Day Adventist Church in Burma Road, just off Independence Avenue.

There are several United Churches of Zambia (UCZ). St Paul's is in Burma Road, just beyond Chibwa Road.

There is a synagogue in Katunjila Road between Freedom Way and Chachacha Road.

The Lusaka Muslim Society Mosque is on the corner of Burma and Changa roads, just off Independence Avenue.

The Hindu temple is easy to see off Independence Avenue, also on Changa Road.

The Sikh temple is in Mumana Road, off Katima Mulilo Road off the Great East Road.

KAFUE NATIONAL PARK

This park was established in 1924. It is the oldest and by far the largest park in the country (22 400 sq km) and one of the largest on the continent.
Location: Central-western Zambia, north and south of the Lusaka-Mongu road.

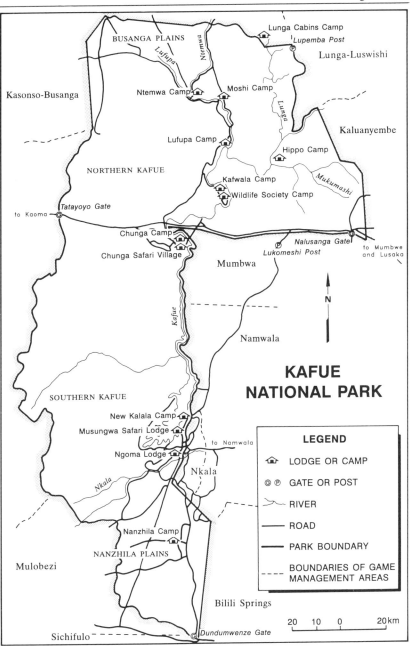

BUSANGA PLAINS

Lufupa

Ntemwa

Lunga Cabins Camp
Lupemba Post
Lunga-Luswishi

Kasonso-Busanga

Ntemwa Camp

Moshi Camp

Lunga

Kaluanyembe

Lufupa Camp

Hippo Camp

NORTHERN KAFUE

Kafwala Camp
Wildlife Society Camp

Mukumashi

to Kaoma

Tatayoyo Gate

Chunga Camp

Nalusanga Gate
Lukomeshi Post

to Mumbwe
and Lusaka

Chunga Safari Village

Mumbwa

Kafue

N

Namwala

KAFUE
NATIONAL PARK

SOUTHERN KAFUE

New Kalala Camp
Musungwa Safari Lodge

to Namwala

Ngoma Lodge

Nkala

Nkala

LEGEND

🏠 LODGE OR CAMP

◎ ℗ GATE OR POST

∿ RIVER

— ROAD

━ PARK BOUNDARY

- - - BOUNDARIES OF GAME
MANAGEMENT AREAS

Nanzhila Camp

NANZHILA PLAINS

Mulobezi

Bilili Springs

20 10 0   20 km

Sichifulo

Dundumwenze Gate

How to get there: From Lusaka follow the main road west to Mumbwa. Here visitors can either turn north if planning to visit camps right in the north, such as Hippo Camp, and camps such as Leopard Lodge and Lunga Cabins in the Lunga Luswishi Game Management Area. Alternatively proceed straight down the main road, which bisects the park. Sixty-six kilometres from Mumbwa on the left is the turnoff to the Itezhi-Tezhi Dam, Musungwa Lodge, Ngoma and the southern Kafue. This is a positively dreadful road, being 115 km of broken tar. The road is being improved by grading away the original tarred surface. Or, again continue along the Mumbwa-Mongu road through the park until the Kafue River bridge. Roads before the bridge go to new camps on the Kafue River. Shortly after the bridge a gate on the north side of the road marks the entry point for Kafwala and Lufupa camps, the road to which proceeds north all the way to the Busanga Plains. A few kilometres further on the tar road, a secondary road turns sharply back south and east to Chunga.

Four-wheel-drive vehicles are not necessary to get as far as Chunga and Lafupa camps in the dry season, but be very cautious if it rains. A four-wheel-drive is definitely necessary to visit the Busanga Plains and the Southern Kafue around Nanzhila.

Most of the interior of the park is inaccessible between November and April-May. Note particularly that many maps show a road from Chunga to Ngoma on the west side of the Kafue River. This is now quite impassable to even the stoutest of four-wheel-drive vehicles and should not be attempted. The only route between the northern and southern sections of the park is the dreadful Musungwa road.

An alternative route to the Kafue that is attractive and adventurous is to come down from the Copperbelt, taking the road that runs from Kitwe to Kasempa via Ingwe. The road from Kitwe to Ingwe is good. Ingwe itself is no more than a village but just beyond it the road crosses the main Solwezi-Kasempa road, at which you turn left to follow a good dirt road to Kasempa. The total distance from Kitwe to Kasempa is about 330 km. From Kasempa there is a reasonable graded track for 98 km to the Lunga Pontoon. Just 16 km before the pontoon turn right down a poor track and 19 km further on is the northernmost gate of the Kafue National Park. Note neither fuel nor supplies are available along this route.

This northern gate can also be reached via a remote and difficult road from Mumbwa. About 160 km from Lusaka the road into Mumbwa is easily visible. Having turned onto it and proceeding north you will see a Total garage on the left as you reach the town. Turn left. This is the last refuelling station in the entire region of the Northern Kafue, so be sure to tank up with a sufficient supply. Proceed down the road in front of the garage and across a stream or gully; then go on up to the crest of the hill where a turnoff on the right is marked by a barely legible sign to Hippo Mine. If you cannot find it ask for the road to the mine or to Chieftainess Kaindu. Follow this track for 31 km then take a left fork to the reform school 9 km beyond that. Be warned that this part of the country is absolutely infested with tsetse flies. Proceed for 21 km to the Kabalushi gate. Don't be surprised if the scouts are tardy about approaching the car – they are staying out of reach of the enormous cloud of tsetses that you will undoubtedly have brought with you. After the gate it is 19 km to the Lubungu pontoon on the Kafue River. The pontoon is usually in operation, but when the water is very low in October/November you have to ford the river on a drift about 2 km upstream. Ask at the village for a guide. The ford is deep but firm and can safely be negotiated in a four-wheel-drive. Leopard Lodge is located on the north bank of the Lubungu River 1 km above the drift.

It is 80 km from the drift to the Lunga Pontoon. Turn left 16 km beyond that and continue for 19 km to the gate. Alternatively, keep left after the pontoon and then left again at the next fork; this road leads eventually to Lunga Cabins, from where it is possible to proceed to Kabalushi gate.

What to see: This reserve takes in a considerable portion of the Kafue River drainage basin. Along the perennial rivers there is beautiful riparian forest, but for the most part it is a flat or very gently undulating landscape of miombo woodland and grassy savanna. For the sake of clarity the park has been divided along the tarred Lusaka-Mongu road into the north Kafue and south Kafue in the description below.

In the south there's miombo, tall mopane forest and Kalahari sand-veld as well as the wonderful, wide Nanzhila Plains of grassland dotted with termite mounds surmounted by baobabs, euphorbias and *diaspyros* trees. The Itezhi-Tezhi Dam is a 370 square km expanse of water along the eastern border of the southern section on which boat cruises offer a different game viewing experience from almost anywhere else in the country.

Vegetation in the northern section of the park is dominated by miombo woodland, termitaria zones and the enormous Busanga floodplains. During the rains the Lufupa River overflows its banks and then as the plains dry massive herds of game are attracted to the grasslands. The ecological diversity of the park as a whole has resulted in probably the widest range of mammal species of any park in the country. Game is reasonably abundant in both north and south although poaching in recent years has, as elsewhere, taken its toll. The area around Lafupa Camp is well known for its predators. Elephants are most likely to be seen near Ngoma in the south, and at Chunga or outside the park in the vicinity of the Lunga pontoon, but it will be some time before they lose their fear and suspicion of people and vehicles. The park is one of the best reserves for antelope in Africa. Roan, sable, Lichtenstein's hartebeest, eland and wildebeest abound on open dambos particularly on the Nanzhila Plains. Impala are prolific in the south as are puku in the north. Oribi abound on the Nanzhila Plains. Sitatunga and red lechwe are confined to the Busanga floodplains and there are said to be yellow-backed duiker in the Ngoma forests. A point of interest is that the waterbuck found in the park are a subspecies, Defassa water-buck, which lack the distinct white ring on the rump belonging to waterbuck elsewhere. There are plenty of predators, especially lions, which are frequently seen on the Busanga, around Lafupa and on the Nanzhila Plains. Lafupa Camp has a reputation for leopard sightings.

Cheetah can be seen on the Nanzhila Plains. Cape hunting or wild dogs are found in the miombo woodlands and the park is considered an important refuge for these threatened animals. Buffalo are more secretive than elsewhere but there are large herds around the Nanzhila and Busanga plains. The Kafue River has an enormous hippo popu-lation. Birding is excellent, especially along the river. Pel's fishing owls are a local speciality. In all over 400 species of birds have been recorded in the park. For further details see the section on birdwatching in chap-ter 5.

Where to stay: The previous government's policy of favouring the Luangwa and allowing other parks, particularly the Kafue, to slide into chaos has meant that the tourist development of the park lags some way behind that of the Luangwa Valley. Poaching was rampant here and the armed forces were themselves responsible for destroying the old established camps like Nanzhila, Ntemwa and Moshi. Nevertheless there are some established camps and a number of new ones are open-ing up in the surrounding Game Management Areas, and between them there are a number of possibilities for accommodation to suit most budgets and tastes. It may be possible to camp in the abandoned lodges, but they are due to be put out to tender for renovation and their status will change, so permission should first be sought from the local NPWS headquarters at Chunga or Ngoma.

The first camp reached from the main road in the North Kafue is Kafwala Camp, which is beautifully situated above a stretch of rapids on the Kafue River and is open only to members of the Wildlife Conservation Society. Temporary membership can be obtained from the society (address given in the section on national parks in chapter 5). Also on the river, a little further northward and some 87 km by road from the tar road, is Lufupa Camp located above a wide and deep stretch of water at the confluence of the Kafue and Lufupa rivers. Lufupa provides fairly basic full board and chalets or camping facilities. Game drives, walks, boating and fishing are optional extras. The camp is justly famous for lion and leopard viewing. Shumba is the only other camp in the north, to the west of the Kafue River. It is located in the Busanga Plains and so is only open in the latter half of the dry season. Both Lufupa and Shumba are booked through Busanga Trails. Most maps show Moshi and Ntemwa camps in the northern part of the park. They were, however, destroyed by the para-military and are currently derelict. Plans are afoot to renovate them.

Hippo Camp is an exclusive tented camp on the national park side of the Kafue River in the north-east. Leopard Lodge is a rather rundown camp on the other bank and outside the park, a few kilometres north of the Lubungu pontoon.

Further north just where the Lunga River flows into the park there is a new lodge, Lunga Cabins, run by Ed and Rona Smythe of African Experience (Pty) Ltd. This is currently the most sophisticated lodge in the Kafue. They offer walking safaris, game drives and boating and fishing trips.

In the southern section of the park accommodation may be divided again into that immediately south of and accessed from the Lusaka-Mongu road and that in the vicinity of Itezhi-Tezhi Dam. Chunga Camp, next door to the local NPWS headquarters, is by far the most easily accessible camp in the Kafue, being only 17 km south of the Lusaka-Mongu road. It is a small, old-style camp picturesquely located on a wide bend in the Kafue River and in a reasonably good area for game. The proximity of the NPWS headquarters detracts just a tiny bit from its tranquillity and beauty. It consists of six rondavels, and camping facilities with very helpful staff who will bring hot water for baths if it is not on tap and even do your cooking. Just across the river in the Game Management Area another luxury lodge is being established by Njovu Safaris.

Then in the south-eastern region of the park the old Ngoma Lodge is under reconstruction. It is also in the midst of the local NPWS headquarters. Musungwa Lodge is the most established lodge in the area and located on a hill with a spectacular view out over the Itezhi-Tezhi Dam. Fuel is available to residents. Nearby is the David Shepherd Camp, which is only open to members of the Wildlife Conservation Society of Zambia or temporary membership holders. Another new camp in the vicinity due to operate from 1994 is Puku Pan.

Nanzhila Camp right in the heart of the Nanzhila Plains is beautifully located but currently derelict. In season a water trailer is left there for users, but if you do obtain permission to camp there, you would be well advised to take your own water and of course all your own provisions. The abandoned buildings are dirty and you would be better off in a tent outside or sleeping on the game viewing platform if you are not unnerved by the frequent passage of lions.

For those particularly interested in walking safaris over a couple of days, Busanga Trails offer them in the northern Kafue and Chundukwa Safaris do walking safaris in the Nanzhila Plains. This is by far the most exciting way of seeing that marvellous area (see chapter 13 for details).

LOWER ZAMBEZI NATIONAL PARK

As yet wild and relatively undeveloped, this is the closest big game reserve to Lusaka and directly opposite Zimbabwe's famous Mana Pools, so more development is likely in the near future.

Location: South-east of Lusaka, the park covers an enormous area between the Zambezi River and the escarpment.

How to get there: The commercial operators (see below and chapter 13) who venture into the park proper at the moment are either based in the vicinity of the Chongwe River – which demarcates the park's western boundary – or enter the park by canoe. The Chongwe River can be accessed from Chirundu along a road for which four-wheel-drive is recommended, crossing the Kafue River by pontoon just beyond Gwabi Lodge. This is the most direct and the usual route into the park. There is another route which is not used by safari operators as yet and requires special permission from the NPWS at Chilanga and is recommended only to the most intrepid of adventurers in very sturdy and reliable four-wheel-drive vehicles. This is to descend the escarpment from the Great East Road via the old Chakwenga mine. The warning above is not given lightly: the going is tough, it is easy to get lost and vehicle failure could more than spoil the holiday. A wildlife scout guide and a second vehicle are advised. Don't even think about going down here during or just after the rainy season. In times past this route was connected to Chirundu via Jecki but that road has been reclaimed by the bush. But if you still insist, take the Great East Road from Lusaka for 106 km till you reach the tsetse fly barrier. About 100 m beyond it a small track turns off to the right. It is 22 km to the park gate and there a road left leads to the scout camp where you are advised to pick up a scout. Return to the gate and proceed down the escarpment. The distance is 80 km and takes four to five hours. The road is good at first but after the first river crossing begins to wind steeply up and down. After the last steep descent a fork indicates a right turn to the now all but lost way through to the Chongwe River and Chirundu, but keep left, turning past a pan and through a tall mopane forest. About 5 km further on at another fork turn right. The left turn here goes all the way to Fira. The right fork leads eventually to an abandoned camp on the banks of the river. Just before the camp a barely visible track leads past the old airfield through a river. After this keep right, beware huge dongas and gullies and make for the river. A last word of warning is that the remote corners of the park are still said to be landmined from the Zimbabwe war.

What to see: This park is a totally magnificent wilderness. Topographically it ranges from the river's edge overhung with huge *diaspyros, ficus* and other riverine species, to a floodplain of treacherous "cotton soil" fringed by mopane forest and interspersed with *Acacia albida* (winterthorn) and then the endlessly climbing hills covered in broad-leafed woodland.

Unfortunately it has been and continues to be poached, particularly for ivory. Elephants are still to be seen in the vicinity of the Chongwe River. There are big herds of buffalo and plenty of lion as well as waterbuck and impala. The river, of course, has hippo and crocodiles. Birdlife is just incredible, specialities being trumpeter hornbills, Meyer's parrot, Lilian's lovebird, and in summer, narina trogon.

Where to stay: The Royal Zambezi Lodge just west of the Chongwe River can accommodate 12 guests in "luxury" tented chalets and offers game drives and walking safaris in the park. Gwabi Lodge is located on the Kafue River, close to its confluence with the Zambezi. Lou and Dale Games of Safari Par Excellance have small exclusive bush camps in the park itself which they access by canoe. Sobek and Tongabezi run canoe safaris which camp en route down the river. Further concessions are in the pipeline and there may be other operators. See chapter 13 for a full list of operators.

BLUE LAGOON NATIONAL PARK

Location: West of Lusaka, on the northern side of the Kafue Flats.

How to get there: Although very close to Lusaka, until recently this park was not open to visitors, as it fell under the preserve of the defence ministry. So it is poorly signposted. Take the Mumbwa road from Lusaka (Route 2), then turn left at a faded blue ZCCM sign approximately 27 km from Lusaka and just opposite a store called the Bancroft Supermarket.

This road leads eventually to the park gate. The gate does not itself mark the real entrance to the park, but you can sign in here before being escorted back the way you have come and down un-signposted roads to the edge of the Kafue Flats.

What to see: This park lies directly opposite Lochinvar National Park on the Kafue Flats. It was started by two doyens of conservation in Zambia, the Critchleys, who farmed here. Although at first the topography seems less attractive than that of Lochinvar, the view when one eventually reaches the flats is quite astounding. A vast, watery plain, as level as a billiard table stretches to the horizon and as far as the eye can see it is just covered with tens of thousands of Kafue lechwe, some buffalo and myriad waterbirds. In the bush behind there are also zebra and other antelope.

Although it is not yet strictly open to the public, do ask to be shown the old Critchley farmhouse. Although unremarkable outside, it has been the special retreat of cabinet ministers and generals and has been immaculately preserved, to the extent that all the old family furniture, silver and photographs remain just as they were when the Critchleys lived there. There are plans to convert this into a tourist lodge. Then ask to see the extraordinary causeway that Mr Critchley built way out into the swamp so that his wife could watch birds. If your vehicle has a tight turning circle drive out along it for a splendid view, but mind the incredible number of huge monitor lizards that live on it. You will marvel at the spirit of endeavour in a bygone age.

Where to stay: There are no facilities or organised safaris at the moment, although this situation is likely to change soon.

The camp that once existed here was destroyed. Visitors signing in will probably be told to camp at the gate. Don't take up this invitation. Ask to be guided down to the abandoned camp at the water's edge. There is a big fig tree nearby which makes for a splendid campsite with all manner of wildlife all around. There's no really dangerous game.

Contact the Zambian Ornithological Society or the Zambian Wildlife Society for more information.

ROUTES (Central Region)

Route 1: Lusaka to Chirundu

Total distance: 137 km. Time: 1,5 hours.
Generally good tar.
Recommended stops: None.
Petrol at Kafue and Chirundu.

The road leaves Lusaka straight from Cairo Road at its south-end circle, but the section out of town is under reconstruction. Until this stretch is finished it will remain rather chaotic.

From Lusaka to the Kafue Bridge is 44 km. There is a good textile market on the right-hand side of the road as you pass through Kafue town. Keep your eyes open for police roadblocks.

From Kafue Bridge the road is good but becomes hilly and winding. Here it is advisable to drive with caution because the huge trucks plying the route have dubious brakes and tend to career down the pass with breathtaking abandon, often with disastrous results. About 4 km from the Siavonga turnoff on the Lusaka side and immediately south of the road lies the Chirundu Fossil Forest, a petrified forest dating back 150 million years. Petrified tree trunks up to 3 m long have become exposed by erosion over millennia. Sporadic finds have also indicated that Middle and Late Stone Age inhabitants of the area used the petrified wood to make tools. It is, of course, strictly against the law to remove fossils or artifacts.

Route 2: Lusaka to Kafue National Park

The M9. Total distance: 276 km. Time: 3,5 hours.

This road is under protracted repair by the Chinese, so look out for detours. Leave Lusaka by taking Kalundwe Road west from Cairo Road past the Soweto market on your left and out through a rather chaotic commercial and industrial area. As you pass the Hindu crematorium on the left the surroundings open out. Shortly thereafter you pass the Garden House Motel on the right. About 27 km from town on the left-hand side there is a turnoff to Blue Lagoon National Park, marked by a rather faded blue ZCCM sign. The road is potholed in places, and particularly badly so in the region before Mumbwa. Keep a lookout for military roadblocks, tsetse fly and African swine fever control barriers.

It is 151 km from Lusaka to Mumbwa. The town lies about 4 km north of the road and is of little consequence other than as the last refuelling stop en route to the Kafue. Mumbwa also marks the turnoff to Hippo Camp, lodges in the Lunga-Luswishi GMA and the road to Kasempa. For these turn left at the Total garage, go down the hill, over a gully and up the next hill at the crest of which the road leads off to the north. If you absolutely have to stay in Mumbwa there is the La Hacienda Hotel. Once run by National Hotels, it does not appear to belong to any one at the moment and although the rooms are reasonably clean with hot water, don't expect food and drink supplies to match the grand pretensions of the menu.

Shortly after Mumbwa a barrier on the road tells you that the Kafue National Park lies to the right of the road and on the left is the clearly signposted road to Musungwa, Itezhi-Tezhi and the south Kafue. The boldness of the signs belies the appalling condition of that road. But from here on the Lusaka-Mongu road is quite good. It is 58 km to the Kafue River Bridge, where there is usually a military roadblock. The guard with his RPG missile launcher will persuade you to stop, but thereafter you can marvel at the view of this enormous river. Shortly after the bridge the road into the northern Kafue is marked by a barrier on the right. The main road proceeds dead straight, bisecting the national park, and it is not uncommon to see game from the road, especially early in the morning. The road to Chunga is signposted some way on. It is 53 km through the park and the end of the reserve is marked again by a picket. For the rest of the road to Mongu see Route 6 in chapter 8.

7 THE SOUTHERN REGION

This is Tongaland. The Tonga people have been living on the northern banks of the Zambezi for almost 1 000 years and their culture is a venerable one, although it was considerably disturbed by the building of Lake Kariba. The most traditional Tonga way of life exists in the hilly region between the lake and the Livingstone-Lusaka road. North of that road until the Kafue Flats Game Management Area the land is fairly developed, particularly in the region of Mazabuka which is rich farming country. The Kafue Flats is, as its name suggests, a vast, almost completely flat country which before the building of the Itezhi-Tezhi Dam was annually flooded by the Kafue River, creating an enormous wetland habitat and wildlife paradise. Farming interests have seen the eradication of big game but it remains a sanctuary for many antelope, in particular the unique Kafue lechwe, some 55 000 of which roam the plains on either side of the Kafue River. Its one of the greatest birding areas in the subcontinent. The best place to see wildlife in the southern region is the Lochinvar National Park. The Kafue National Park extends right down into the southern region and can be accessed from Kalomo (see Route 4), but is dealt with under Central Region. The other attractions in the southern region are Livingstone and the Victoria Falls and Lake Kariba itself. The Zambian shore of the lake does not have the game that Zimbabwe does and the only development has taken place near the dam wall on the eastern side of the lake at Siavonga and at the fishing town of Sinazongwe.

LIVINGSTONE AND THE VICTORIA FALLS

The Victoria Falls is arguably the most famous tourist attraction in southern Africa, unquestionably one of the great wonders of the world and reason alone to visit Zambia. (The view up the gorge from the Zambian bank is considered by many to be more spectacular than that seen from Zimbabwe.) It is 1 690 m across, has an average height of 92 m, and when in flood discharges as much as 546 million litres of water a minute. But the statistics are unimportant: the mighty cascade of the Zambezi River as it plunges into the Batoka Gorge in the widest curtain of falling water on the planet remains, even to frequent visitors, a spectacle of quite epiphanic proportions.

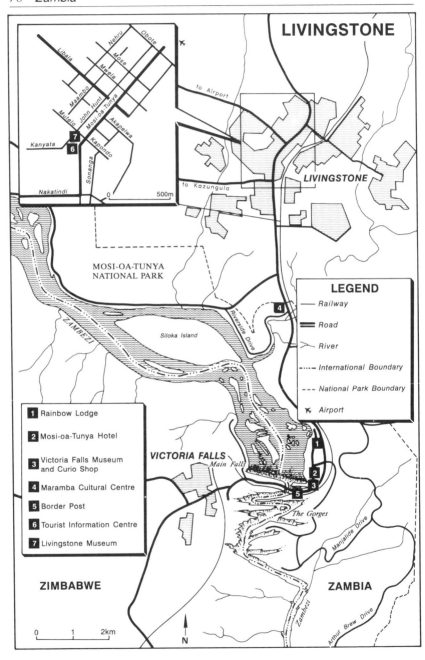

LIVINGSTONE

to Airport

LIVINGSTONE

to Kazungula

MOSI-OA-TUNYA
NATIONAL PARK

Siloka Island

Riverside Drive

LEGEND

— Railway

▬ Road

⤬ River

····· International Boundary

--- National Park Boundary

⤧ Airport

1 Rainbow Lodge

2 Mosi-oa-Tunya Hotel

3 Victoria Falls Museum
and Curio Shop

4 Maramba Cultural Centre

5 Border Post

6 Tourist Information Centre

7 Livingstone Museum

VICTORIA FALLS
Main Falls

The Gorges

Manjalide Drive

ZIMBABWE

ZAMBIA

Zambezi

Arthur Brew Drive

0   1   2km

N

Inset map streets: Libala, Nehru, Obote, Mose, Mwela, Maambo, John Hunt, Mosi-oa-Tunya, Akapelwa, Mutelo, Kapondo, Kanyata, **7**, **6**, Sonanga, Nakatindi, 0   500m

The force of the water as it pours with a roar into the chasm causes great gusts of air to shoot a curtain of spray high into the air that can be seen from up to 30 km away which gave rise to the Falls' original name of Mosi-oa-tunya, "the smoke that thunders". So it was called when David Livingstone was lead to it by Sekeletu of the Makokolo on 16 November 1854, and he named it after his queen.

The first European settlement at the falls was located a mile upstream on the north bank at the old drift where people and goods crossed the Zambezi prior to the building of the railway and bridge (see: What to see and do on page 82). In 1904 a new township was laid out and the town of Livingstone established on its present site.

Livingstone is an attractive, sleepy town. Colonial houses with corrugated iron roofs and deep verandas recline beneath the deep shade of mango trees; the central business area is small yet spaciously set astride the wide Mosi-oa-tunya Road. Two very attractive buildings from the art-deco era hold their own against more recent and considerably uglier architecture and the back streets such as Kuta Way are a living memorial to African commerce of an earlier era.

Livingstone is not unsafe but first-time visitors are likely to be put off by insistent and shady money changers and horrible little urchins who will attempt to wash your car. If you ignore them they will "wash" it anyway and then demand money for the dubious service of having rendered it more dirty than it was before. An instant, firm and smiling refusal is the best policy. Changing money in the bank is more time-consuming but infinitely safer than on the street. Car theft is not the problem that it is in Lusaka and the Copperbelt, but don't leave a packed car unattended.

Access

By air: Livingstone International Airport is located close to town off Libala Drive. Although an international airport, it receives few international flights. Regional Air used to fly direct from Johannesburg, and may resume these flights in the future. There are no flights between Livingstone and Lusaka on Aero Zambia, and visitors should book charter flights for this route. Chartered passengers can land and clear customs at Livingstone. Consider the option of flying to Victoria Falls in Zimbabwe and hitching a ride to the border.

By train: The railway station is located close to Mosi-oa-Tunya Road, just south of the CBD. The rail runs from Lusaka. Goods trains come from south of the border, but in the unlikely event of visitors arriving this way, they will probably not have the patience to actually wait and cross the border by train rather than on foot. In any case most visitors would disembark at the border and the falls because most accommodation on the Zambian side is located there.

Highly exclusive package train journeys being developed in South Africa operate occasional journeys across the Zambezi.

By bus: Most coaches to and from Lusaka disembark outside the New Fairmount Hotel right in town.

By car: Livingstone is 480 km from Lusaka on a reasonable tar road. The main road passes through Livingstone as Mosi-oa-tunya Road, linking Zambia with Zimbabwe over the famous Victoria Falls Bridge. The bridge marks the border and a more spectacular frontier would be hard to find. Alas, clearing customs at this border post is a tiresome and tedious process. For some reason once immigration has been completed at the border, you are required to report to the immigration office, which is halfway to town and instantly recognisable by the number of trucks parked outside. There you will be pushed around from office to office before getting an import permit, which costs a few dollars. Then you have to go to the State Insurance offices in town (on the left just beyond the tourist information office) to get third-party insurance. All of this takes a great deal of time and woe betide the traveller arriving before or after hours or during lunchtime. Fortunately day visitors need not subject themselves to this procedure.

Access from Botswana is accomplished by crossing the pontoon at Kazungula, whence one approaches town on a good tar road from Mambova. The road becomes Nakatindi Road when it reaches town.

From Namibia the conventional route from Katima Mulilo is to cross the Zambezi by ferry to Sesheke and then proceed via Mambova to join the route described above. The tar road between Sesheke and Mambova has collapsed into an appalling succession of potholes which are agony to negotiate. So at all times other than during high rains when the Namibian stretch is itself hazardous, it's preferable to proceed via Botswana and the Kazungula ferry. If one can bear the thought of so many borders and has a multiple entry visa (if needed) for Zimbabwe, then going that way and through Victoria Falls offers substantially better roads and even the chance of seeing game.

Tourist information

The Zambian National Tourist Board has an office that is easily spotted between the museum and the civic centre right where Mosi-oa-tunya Road bends into the CBD. Its staff are friendly but not always well informed. Ask for the tourist map of Livingstone and Victoria Falls, which is a useful if dated guide. If they don't have one it may be available from the map office at the Department of Surveys, located across the road in a grimy corridor between the bank and the travel agent.

Accommodation

(See chapter 12 for full details.) As the town of Livingstone is 11 km from Victoria Falls, the majority of visitors will probably opt for accommodation closer to the Falls themselves, usually choosing between the Intercontinental Hotel and the Rainbow Lodge. The former is the more luxurious and a mere 300 m from the lip of the Falls, whereas the latter is really a motel with thatch chalets and a terrace bar that commands a magnificent view of the river. If staying at the Intercontinental do avail yourself of the offer of breakfast at the Falls edge – it's magnificent. In town there's the New Fairmount Hotel and Chalets Motel.

For exclusivity Tongabezi, 17 km upstream, provides accommodation in the ultimate combination of rusticity and sophistication. Booking is essential. There's an office for Tongabezi in the shops where Nakatindi Road joins Mosi-oa-tunya Road. Transfers from town and airport are arranged; otherwise take Nakatindi Road for approximately 25 km, turning left at the sign. Tongabezi offers guests canoeing, walking and safaris, rafting, picnics on Livingstone Island, flights over the Falls and more. Chundukwa Safaris have a similar but more low-key lodge 30 km upriver offering canoeing safaris and walking safaris in the Kafue National Park. And just a little further on is Kubu Cabins whose huge advertisement adorns one wall of the customs house. This is a new, upper-middle range lodge promising excellent food, timber and thatch chalets and a quiet stretch of river with boating trips, package visits to the Falls, canoeing with Makora Quest and various other activities. They also have a quiet and attractive campsite.

Camping facilities are undersupplied. The Rainbow Lodge has a campsite which is convenient but far from pleasant and less than safe. Sobek are developing better facilities; enquire at their offices. Busika

Farms, 10 km outside Livingstone (follow the signs from Katete Avenue on the northern side of town), are developing a game farm with basic camping facilities away from all the hustle and bustle. There is also a guesthouse sleeping eight for larger parties of self-catering travellers, and two rustic wooden chalets adjacent to the farmhouse.

What to see and do

The Victoria Falls

Top priority of course is seeing the Falls, which is now possible from almost every vantage point imaginable. The best time of year is probably not during the high-water period of March to May. Awesome as the sheer volume of the deluge then is, the spray that falls like rain from a height of almost a kilometre all but masks from sight the Falls themselves. Likewise the spectacle is somewhat lessened at lowest water during November/December. Generally, but especially when the water is high, it's advisable to take a raincoat and waterproof bags for cameras and waterproof shoes or sandals. The spray can drench you in minutes. The spray or "rain" has created a wonderful rainforest along the Falls' edge which – particularly on the Zimbabwean side where it is somewhat better preserved – hosts plant species that would not otherwise survive in the surrounding dry climate, as well as bushbuck, monkeys and baboons and a plethora of birds and insects.

There are numerous points from which you can view the Falls. On the Zambian side they are reached by a small road that turns off just above the customs post. Or walk down past the Mosi-oa-tunya Intercontinental Hotel. Paved paths lead to various lookout points at which the absence of barriers or protective railing adds to both scenic and thrill value. Ideally try to see the Falls from both sides of the border, for which one-day visas will be issued to those needing them. Zambia offers views of the Eastern Cataract, a great view up the main gorge (especially at sunset) and terrific views from the Knife Edge Bridge of both the Falls and down the gorge below the magnificent railway bridge. The bridge was completed in 1905 as part of the grand design of a railway line from Cape Town to Cairo. Crossing the Victoria Falls Bridge is an experience in itself. This is surely one of the world's great frontiers; the Zimbabwean side offers the rainforest and a walk to precipitous Danger Point and the deluge over Devil's Cataract, above which is sited Livingstone's statue and monument. Incidentally the statue is incorrectly sited for the explorer first saw the falls from the opposite bank. Do go and look at the Falls at different times of day, as they are never quite the same. Try to go at night as well (but not unaccompanied), especially if there is a moon when you might see a lunar rainbow and the Falls assume a powerful and primordial mystique.

Other viewing points on the Zambian side are from down in the Boiling Pot or from the ancient baobab, the Look Out Tree, that stands beyond the railway line opposite Rainbow Lodge.

The Batoka Gorge is well worth seeing. It is the beginning of the huge Zambezi Valley, which stretches all the way to the gorge at Cahora Basa in Mozambique and remains one of the wildest and most beautiful places in Africa. Sadly, although the Batoka Gorge is scenically spectacular and a wildlife paradise, it is threatened by the building of another dam. Not only will this destroy a unique habitat and breeding ground for many raptors, including some very rare species, it will certainly wreck some of the activities listed below. Protests have been lodged from many quarters but so far they have fallen on deaf ears.

Activities associated with the Falls are a boat trip in the Boiling Pot and white water rafting as well as plane flips, the so-called "flight of angels". (For details see chapter 13.)

The Victoria Falls have become famous for probably the most exciting but safe white-water rafting in the world and for many a visit would not be complete without doing the one-day run down the Batoka Gorge. Two companies operate from the Zambian side and have the advantage over Zimbabwean operators of being able to start right from the Boiling Pot.

Experienced guides pilot inflatable rafts down a series of awesome rapids interspersed with pools whose tranquillity belies their inevitable slide into a further tumult of white water. The gorge itself is beautiful, the skies above filled with numerous birds – especially raptors – and the waters below with crocodiles and other exciting nasty things. Rafting doesn't require extraordinary fitness, only the capability to walk down the gorge and back out again at the end.

The so-called "float of the angels" is a non white-water boat ride around the Boiling Pot.

Batoka Sky offers a "flight of the angels" in two-seater microlights and perhaps the most spectacular aerial vantage of the Falls.

Tongabezi, Makora Quest and Chundukwa Safaris offer canoe safaris on the Zambezi above the Falls, which include camping or picnics and game viewing on islands in the river.

Other places to see

The Mosi-oa-tunya zoological park – a very small but scenically attractive game reserve with lovely riverine trees and a variety of animals that can be seen at reasonably close quarters. (Tourist brochures credit the park with all sorts of species but many of these have sadly long since departed via Livingstone kitchens.) Rather mismanaged in the past, it is currently being refenced to accommodate white rhino. There is no other big game although very occasionally elephants cross over from Zimbabwe. Do stop at the Old Drift cemetery, which is a poignant remnant of the first European settlement. Before the rail bridge all people and goods crossed the river at this point and the first settler, one F J Clarke, arrived in 1898 to trade and start a hotel. By 1903 the European population was 68. But the settlement was ill-sited in a flat and marshy area and lost many of its inhabitants to malaria. Here they remained buried when the town was moved to healthier ground at the coming of the railway in 1904. About 500 m downstream of the cemetery a monument marks the site of the old drift.

The Livingstone Museum, located just behind the tourist centre, is well worth a visit. It is Zambia's national museum and has informative archaeological and ethnographic displays. Its premier exhibit is a collection of letters, notes and other paraphernalia that belonged to David Livingstone. There is a natural history section in which the most interesting exhibit shows the three different kinds of lechwe found in Zambia. The entry fee is US $5, children free. There is also a dull craft shop.

The Railway Museum off Chishimba Falls Road has a large collection of old trains, but is far more interesting for its collection of old photographs which graphically illustrate the trials and tribulations of pioneer days. Adults US $5, children free.

The Victoria Falls Field Museum is located just above the Falls themselves, adjacent to the Intercontinental Hotel and it is built over an archaeological site that has uncovered evidence of early hominids who lived in the area as far back as 2,5 million years ago.

Next door to the Field Museum is a curio shop in which a number of craft sellers tout their wares. Products are of reasonable quality but the competition for your patronage can be exhausting.

The Maramba Cultural Village between the Falls and Livingstone purports to give visitors a fascinating glimpse of Zambian culture, but it is dull and tacky. However cultural dancing is a regular event that could prove temporarily distracting.

If all the above has failed to excite you, a last sure way to get an adrenalin rush is to leap off the Victoria Falls Bridge with a rubber cord around your ankles and bounce sickeningly up and down under the expert guidance of Quest Bungie Jumpers (details in chapter 13).

LAKE KARIBA

Below the Victoria Falls and the Batoka Gorge the Zambezi has carved a wide, deep valley that for centuries was a major impediment to exploration and trade to the north. Then in 1955 the government of the then Federation of Rhodesia and Nyasaland decided to dam the Zambezi. The site chosen was the Kariba Gorge, where the mighty river was constricted through an arched gap of solid rock about 100 m wide. Shaped like a giant fish trap, Kariba is named after the "kariwa" (Shona) or "kariba" (Makorere), a small trap for catching birds and mice. Apparently in days gone by a great slab of rock overhung the gorge that resembled such a device, but on a giant scale.

The contract was awarded to an Italian company, Impresit, which began work in November 1956. The surrounding country was so rugged that the site could only be reached along centuries-old elephant trails. On 22 June 1959 the last skip of concrete was poured. The result was a wall 128 m high, 600 m across, 26 m thick at its base and 13 m wide at the top that holds back the might of the Zambezi for 280 km and tamed at last, against all predictions, the legendary river god Nyaminyami.

The story of Nyaminyami's struggle against the forces of the 20th century is integral to the mythology of Kariba and one cannot look at the wall and the vast waters behind it without knowing a little of its legendary history. For centuries prior to the damming the Zambezi Valley was inhabited by the BaTonga, an essentially hunter-gatherer people who lived in a symbiotic relationship with the teeming wildlife of the valley. According to their folklore this existence was presided over by a benevolent spirit and guardian of the river, who is depicted as a kind of giant snake and was called Nyaminyami. The Tonga elders protested against the building of the wall and refused to leave their ancestral grounds. The tribes even took up arms to prevent their removal, but their bows and arrows could hardly match firearms and after several tribesmen had been killed they reluctantly departed at gunpoint. The elders prophesied, however, that Nyaminyami would destroy the dam. No one associated with the project has ever forgotten just how nearly this did in fact happen. In 1957 the river rose a colossal 100 feet as 3,5 million gallons of water surged through the gorge every second, flooding the coffer dam and setting back the works. The Zambezi has a double flood regimen from local and distant rains. This time, as usual, they followed one another but did not coincide. The following year, at odds of one in a thousand, the river flooded again. Both local and distant catchment areas received unusually heavy rains. As had never happened before the runoff plunged into the Zambezi Valley all at the same time and the combined floodwaters smashed down on the emerging wall in the greatest tide the river dwellers had ever known.

Nyaminyami threw everything he could muster against the project, causing extensive damage and washing away a whole section of wall. In all 17 men lost their lives building Kariba; some of those men are now embalmed forever in the one million cubic metres of concrete into which they slipped and with which Nyaminyami was finally subdued.

The building of Kariba generated many other stories of heroism and endeavour. One that caught the imagination of the world was Operation Noah, in which thousands of animals were rescued from the rising waters.

The primary function of Kariba is to generate hydro-electric power. Ten turbine generators produce a combined output of 1 350 megawatts of electricity, supplying both Zimbabwe and Zambia. A second major industry was introduced in the form of a small sardine-like fish from lake Tanganyika.

These "kapenta", as they are known, multiplied exceedingly rapidly in the early nutrient-rich years of the dam and today the lights of the commercial fishing boats used to lure big shoals into their nets can be seen spread right across the lake at night. But perhaps the most successful industry on the lake now is tourism. The Zimbabwean side, where the herds of game have been preserved, is a much more desirable tourist destination. On the Zambian side almost every living wild thing has long since been eaten, and the tourist industry centres on watersports and game fishing at Siavonga and to a lesser extent at Sinazongwe.

SIAVONGA

How to get there: The road to Siavonga turns off the Lusaka-Chirundu road just 18 km from Chirundu. It is 65 km of reasonable tar road winding alternately through pretty hills and the rather overgrazed settlements of the Tonga people. One is likely to be offered great big lumps of amethyst and other semi-precious rock along the way.

What to see: Siavonga is Zambia's premier "seaside" town. Primarily a weekend destination from Lusaka and for the innumerable conferences to which the Zambian bureaucracy retire at the drop of a hat, Siavonga may with a certain stretch of the imagination be said to resemble a slightly sleazy Mediterranean resort. As most of the lakeshore trees have been cut down and the game long since shot out, Siavonga cannot offer the immediate attractions of Kariba in Zimbabwe. Nevertheless there is the possibility of exciting fishing on the lake and a laid-back atmosphere with a magnificent view across the waters to the blue hills of Matusadona in Zimbabwe. Consider Siavonga as a first or last stop en route to Zimbabwe or as a stopover while exploring the remote and winding roads of Tongaland between Livingstone and Chirundu.

Although the main attractions are fishing and lazing in the sun, there is a crocodile farm just outside town where for a very small fee, visitors can examine enclosures full of beady-eyed proto-handbags. And of course there is the Kariba Dam wall, which has been described above. The turnoff to the dam wall and border post is clearly marked.

Where to stay: There is a wide choice if not variety of places to stay in Siavonga. The Manchinchi Bay Lodge is probably the most attractively positioned of the three main lodges, but otherwise similar to the Zambezi Lodge and Lake Kariba Inn. For budget and self-catering travellers Eagles Rest Chalets are recommended. Accommodation is simple but comfortable and the setting is beautiful. To get there, take the left fork at the entrance to the Manchinchi Bay Lodge. Another budget facility, the Leisure Bay Motel, is currently being renovated.

SINAZONGWE

This is the only other major development on the Zambian shores of Lake Kariba. It is primarily a harbour for the kapenta fishing industry and has little to offer tourists. Gwembe Safaris have a 45-ft houseboat moored here that is available for hire.

LOCHINVAR NATIONAL PARK

Location: Lochinvar lies south of the Kafue River where it floods over the vast Kafue Flats and just a short distance to the north of the Lusaka-Livingstone road.

How to get there: Proceed to Monze from Lusaka or Livingstone as described in Route 3. From Monze the road is clearly signposted. It is 44 km long and rather rough so a four-wheel-drive is recommended, although not strictly necessary in the dry season.

What to see: The Kafue Flats are covered in places by vast stretches of water or lagoons which attract vast flocks of birds, including many species not found in large numbers elsewhere. Otherwise rare birds such as the wattled crane appear in flocks of hundreds in the summer.

Although the park does not have big game other than buffalo and hippo, there is a large variety of antelope, in particular thousands and thousands of Kafue lechwe which occur only on these floodplains. To see these herds and the skeins of birds that seem to rise and fall continually over the water is just enthralling.

The Kafue Flats have been designated a wetland of international importance under the Ramsar Convention by the IUCN and the World Wide Fund for Nature (WWF), who have sponsored a management project for the area that attempts to give local people an interest in conservation both through redistribution of tourist revenue and controlled harvesting of natural resources. Visitors will at first be surprised to see fishermen in the park, but they will soon realise that as they pole their *mokoros* across the swamp they are very much a part of a unique and fascinating ecosystem. The Zambia wetlands scheme is in many ways a pilot project for future wildlife conservation in Africa which recognises the interdependence of humans and wildlife. Enquire at the gate or at the lodge for the leaflets explaining the project as well as the bird checklist published by the WWF and ZOS, which lists the 428 bird species found at Lochinvar.

There are two national monument sites in the park that are worth seeing as much for their scenic value as their historical importance. The Gwisho Hot Springs are well signposted and lie about a kilometre west of the lodge.

Archaeological digging in the 1960s showed that the low mounds around the spring result from Late Stone Age habitation on the site between the second and third millennia BC. Several skeletons of these early inhabitants were discovered in the excavation giving detailed evidence of their hunter-gatherer lifestyles. Nowadays game comes to lick tentatively at the salts deposited where the sulphurous waters seep and trickle into lush meadows at the edge of the Kafue Flats. On the top of Sebanzi Hill, which is clearly visible from the springs, is the site of an Iron Age village which has been shown to have been inhabited for most of the last 1 000 years. Not much remains to be seen but the view over the surrounding flats is dramatic. The thick bush at the base of the hill is the most likely place to find Lochinvar's elusive herds of buffalo.

Where to stay: There are two options. The park runs a modest, pleasant campsite where a few chalets are being built.

Better known is Lochinvar Lodge, which is the original farmhouse. Run to date by the parastatal NHDC, it has unfortunately become very tacky. The rooms are fairly clean with en-suite facilities and the food is very basic. An astronomical sum is asked for this third-grade fare, but the staff are willing to acknowledge its shortcomings and it is possible to bargain down prices considerably. However, when this becomes privately run as is planned it may become one of the premier destinations in the country. Watch this space.

ROUTES (Southern Region)

Route 3: Lusaka to Livingstone

Total distance: 472 km. Time: 5,5 hours.
All roads are tarred.
Recommended stops: Tonga craft museum, Choma; or overnight at Lochinvar National Park or Wildlives Game Farm.
Petrol at Kafue, Mazabuka, Monze and Choma.

The road out of Lusaka is being upgraded but most of the way to the bridge over the Kafue has been completed and is now a smooth drive. 11,5 km from the bridge turn right at the clearly signposted junction. A reasonably good road winds pleasantly through undulating country until Mazabuka, when the great Kafue Flats suddenly open out before you. Beware quarry blasting in the hills. Mazabuka is a pleasant farming town with a pre-war feel. Between Mazabuka and Monze the road deteriorates and is under reconstruction. In Monze large signboards proclaim the turnoff to Lochinvar Lodge. Note that the Lochinvar access road is poor and unsuitable for ordinary vehicles in the wet season. Of historical interest, at the south end of town a sign points right to the old Fort Monze and cemetery, one of the earliest police posts in the territory. Only a mound of earth, a commemorative plaque and nearby graves remain. The site is 16 km from town on a dry-season-only road.

It's 97 km from Monze to Choma on a good tar road. Wildlives Game Farm, 15 km before Choma, offers basic camping facilities. Gwembe Safaris have a few chalets and a secure campsite in town (see chapter 12). As one enters Choma, directly opposite the BP petrol station on the Lusaka side of town is the Tonga Craft Museum. This is definitely the place to stop, stretch your legs, get a snack to eat and see the best craft display in the country. Permanent and temporary exhibitions are housed in a beautifully restored old school. A shop sells local and other African crafts of excellent quality.

After Choma the road leaves the Kafue Flats and deteriorates, becoming badly potholed as it passes into gently undulating woodland country for about 70 km to Kalomo. Do keep a lookout just 3 km before Kalomo, where the road bisects a gentle mound. This is the Kalundu Mound and although apparently insignificant it has considerable archaeological importance.

It is an Iron Age site dating perhaps as far back as 300 AD, and was formed by the accumulation of refuse and rubble for a thousand years thereafter. Kalomo is a town of little note except for a delightful corrugated iron house on stilts and the local magistrate's house, which was the residence of the former Administrator of North-western Rhodesia between 1903 and 1907. Unfortunately it is not open to the public. It is about 115 km from here to Livingstone and the road leads eventually down into the Zambezi Valley and straight into Mosi-oa-tunya Road.

Route 4: Livingstone to Kafue National Park via Ndumdumwenzi Gate

Distance: between 200 and 300 km depending on destination. Time: 3 hours to gate then a further 2-3 hours to Ngoma.
Dry season only. Four-wheel-drive recommended.
Petrol at Kalomo, but not always reliable.

Take the Lusaka road by following Mosi-oa-tunya Road northwards out of Livingstone. It is tar for about 115 km to Kalomo, where a rusty sign to the Kafue National Park directs you left through the village past a government services depot. At the fork keep left and then bear left again at the next fork. It is 75 km to the national park. The road is a little bumpy and sandy, but reasonable and proceeds through rural Tonga villages for an hour before climbing through a range of wooded hills and then descending to Ndumdumwenzi Gate. Sign in. It's approximately 100 km to Ngoma or 60 km to the deserted camp of Nanzhila. Permission to stay here must have been obtained from the NPWS at Chilanga or the regional HQ at Ngoma – it will not be given at the gate, if it will be given at all. The road proceeds into the most beautiful mopane and baobab woodland and is good in the dry season, but could be treacherous if wet. Then the Nanzhila Plains open up to the west. Keep right if proceeding to Ngoma. A left fork takes one to Nanzhila Camp across the plains, on which the dried and cracked mud makes for very uncomfortable travelling. It is necessary to go through Ngoma and the riverbed east of the camp to proceed up the main road to Musungwa Lodge and the Itezhi-Tehzi Dam.

Other options in the southern region for the exploration-minded are: The road from Monze to Namwala and Ngoma, which is a possible alternative route to the South Kafue from the Mumbwa road. The byroads that wind through Tongaland between Siavonga and Sinazongwe pass through some breathtaking landscape where elephants are still said to roam. Sturdy vehicles are recommended for both options.

8 THE WESTERN REGION

Between its source right in the very north-western tip of the country and the Victoria Falls, the Zambezi River grows from a trickle to one of the mightiest rivers on the continent.

Although it has barely influenced the wider topography because it has not eroded the kind of deep valley that the Luangwa has in the east, it goes without saying that the Zambezi is the focus of all life in the region. It is the principal reason for tourists to visit the area, and even if it is not, it will certainly be a major influence on their travels there.

Western Zambia is predominantly Lozi-speaking, being the traditional kingdom of Bulozi or Barotseland. In north-western Zambia the people are Lunda or Luvale (see Population, chapter 1).

This is probably the least developed region in the country and the most difficult to explore. Although Mongu, the administrative capital of North-western Province, and Senanga can be reached in ordinary cars along reasonable tar roads from Lusaka, a four-wheel-drive vehicle will be essential for wider exploration, particularly west of the river. Tourist destinations include three remote national parks, the Barotse floodplain and the course of the great river itself.

BAROTSELAND

The ancient kingdom of Barotseland covered almost the entire region, but its traditional heart has always been the fertile plains annually flooded by the Zambezi. Such a large river would have cut a deep valley for itself aeons ago were it not for the presence of several hard basalt dykes that lie across the river's path. The Victoria Falls are the last and most dramatic of these, but several others upstream hold back both the waters and the deep Kalahari sands – with profound implications for navigation, transport and settlement in the area. Archaeological finds have shown that Bantu settlement on the upper Zambezi dates back at least three centuries before Christ and San (Bushman) habitation goes back tens of thousands of years before that. However, the forefathers of today's Lozi people are thought to have migrated down from the region of central Zaïre in about the 17th century, conquering or assimilating those who had preceded them.

Although early central African kingdoms such as the Lozi traded with other kingdoms and thence the outside world, it was only in 1798 that Europe began to take an active interest in the region when a Brazilian named Jose de Assumpcao e Mello penetrated as far as Luvale country in what is today north-western Zambia. From the middle of the 19th century a succession of missionaries, traders and rogues began to explore the territory. The Portuguese were by then well established in Angola and began to make moves eastwards with the ultimate goal of uniting east and west Portuguese Africa.

In 1849 a Portuguese trader, Silva Antonio Francisco Porto, based himself in Barotseland. The next European to enter the territory was a Hungarian named Lazlo Maygar, who passed through the Mwinilunga district in 1851. It is a fascinating insight into David Livingstone's character that he had the opportunity to meet Maygar but deliberately chose not to, so that he would not have to mention him in his diaries and thus refer to any European penetration prior to his own. As for Silva Porto, his story is a fascinating one. He continued to live and trade in the area right up until 1890, when his village was attacked. He was so mortified by this sign of rejection from the people among whom he had settled that he wrapped himself up in the Portuguese flag, lay down on 13 barrels of gunpowder and blew himself through the roof of his house; only dying (from shock) the next day.

On Livingstone's return journey from Loanda (Luanda) in 1855 he was shown and named the Victoria Falls and following its announcement to the world a succession of traders and missionaries began to move over the Zambezi. Primary among these was a hunter and trader named George Westbeech who came to Barotseland in 1871, apparently with a toothbrush in the band of his hat. Westbeech said that it represented the only bit of civilisation that he had and that he wanted. His influence at the Lozi court, then situated at Sesheke, saw to it that Francois Coillard and the Paris Evangelical Mission became established in Barotseland.

It was a time of considerable politicking for the Lozi throne. The Kololo, Sotho migrants from southern Africa, had been established as overlords over the Lozi for half a century, but under the leadership of one Sepopa the Lozi throne was restored when in a single bloody night the Lozi rose up and slew every single Kololo, including women and children.

Interestingly however the original Lozi language has disappeared and it is the Sotho language of the Kololo that Lozis have retained as their own. When the missionary Fred Arnot stayed at Lealui, blood still flowed rather freely and he reported a veritable "Golgotha of skulls". He witnessed the sort of events that coloured the Victorian English perception of central Africa. Important occasions or objects were sanctified with human blood by chopping off a child victim's fingers and toes, then sprinkling the blood over the boat or object before ripping open the child's guts and throwing them into the river. Alternatively, victims were staked out at ant nests to be eaten alive. In 1885 a former claimant to the throne called Lubosi returned to drive out his usurper. To make sure that this time he stayed on the throne he purged the land of any other claimant's supporters. Westbeech witnessed it and described how every man and woman who surrendered was disembowelled or had their limbs smashed and were then left to die of starvation. Children were simply fed to the crocodiles.

Lubosi called himself Lewanika and it was he that the British South Africa Company deceived into giving away the mineral rights that eventually led Britain to formally take over Barotseland as a protectorate in 1900.

Today's king of the Lozi is Lewanika's grandson. He is known as His Royal Highness the Litunga Ilute Yeta IV. Although blood has long since ceased to be the currency of life in Barotseland, the Lozi are a proud nation who pledge allegiance to the king and insist that their protectorate status prior to Zambia's independence in 1964 entitles their kingdom to its own independence now. This is an ongoing political issue which visitors are likely to read a lot about in the Zambian press. The greatest display of Lozi tradition is marked in the annual *Kuomboka* ceremony (see Festivals and cultural events, chapter 5).

From a visitor's point of view the centre of Barotseland is the great Barotse floodplain. At Sioma the Ngonye Falls mark the basalt dyke that is the lynchpin of the entire floodplain. The basalt has checked the erosive power of the Zambezi, and at the end of every rainy season causes the great tide of water that washes down from the Angolan highlands to flood the river's banks and turn the surrounding grasslands into an inland sea.

The Barotse floodplain stands in marked contrast to most of the rest of the country because the otherwise ubiquitous woodland gives way to wide open grasslands. Years ago Lozi custom prevented the killing of lechwe other than by royal consent and the plains were covered with enormous herds of game. Alas, as elsewhere the country's independence saw the erosion of that kind of authority and today the only herds remaining are those of Nguni cattle. Through the middle of the plains runs the great river, here and there diverted into oxbow lagoons and creeks. Mango trees are sporadically dotted like dark green islands on the yellow plain and the rather beautiful reed huts of Lozi villages nestle into their deep shade. It is a pastoral landscape, but its timelessness is paradoxically bound fast to the caprices of the seasons. When the river floods the villagers must retreat to higher ground.

When it again subsides they can return to plant the refertilised land and graze their cattle on regenerated pastures. The change is exceptionally striking. At the end of the dry season the river has shrunk to a single channel. In March it suddenly begins to rise and within weeks what was a dusty yellow plain is transformed into an inland sea with horizons of green and azure. Where previously one could walk and drive, boats become the only transport. Even quite large craft like the Zambezi post boat steam up and down, connecting towns hundreds of kilometres apart.

With such water it is obvious that angling is another major reason to visit Barotseland. And conveniently the fishing here is at its best just when it is deteriorating elsewhere. In June and July the floodwaters begin to recede, bringing back both the fish that have spread over the floodplain to the more concentrated waters of the main channel and the nutrients they eat. For the deep-water predator fish such as tigerfish this signals a time of great feeding activity and consequently it is an excellent time to catch them. Fishing safaris to the region are becoming increasingly popular and there are an increasing number of companies offering such safaris (see chapter 13).

However, for visitors who cannot afford that and do not have their own boat, there are numerous fishermen who will be more than willing to take you out on their dugouts for a small fee. Whether for fishing or simply for a sunset cruise this surpasses a ride in a powerboat any day and is a highly recommended experience.

Unlike fish, game resources have considerably diminished in the region in recent years and in spite of the fact that the whole country west of the Zambezi has been declared a game management area, visitors cannot expect to see much outside the two major national parks. Even hippos have all but disappeared. But the apparent scarcity of crocodiles should not be taken as an invitation to swim.

Birdlife is excellent, though, and its abundance can be attributed to Lozi traditional law which protected all birds and their eggs – with special protection afforded to egrets, marabou storks, white-bellied storks and vultures.

Birdlife also responds to the flood regimen, moving away during the floods but returning in huge flocks to feed on the exposed banks and shallow pools when the waters begin to recede.

Mongu

This is both the regional capital and commercial hub of the province. It is close to Lealui and Limulunga, the Litunga's palaces, and therefore the seat of the provincial administration. Set on a hill that rises relatively high above the surroundings, Mongu commands a wide prospect out over the floodplains, but the Zambezi itself lies several kilometres to the west and the view is unspectacular. It might seem peculiar then that Mongu has a harbour, but this is connected to the Zambezi by an 8 km-long channel.

There is not a great deal to see but a worthwhile excursion is to go down to the palace at Lealui where there is a museum outlining the great Lozi heritage. The ramshackle fishermen's village at the harbour is perhaps the most photogenic part of the town although the tremendous poverty associated with it is a little depressing.

There are three hotels, details of which are given in chapter 12. Petrol and supplies are available and vehicle repairs and some parts can be found. Be careful, however, of local mechanics abusing your dependency on them with exorbitant prices.

Senanga

Some 95 km south on the tar road from Mongu, this is a smaller and more attractive village also set on a small hill, but unlike Mongu the Zambezi flows by immediately beneath it. Consequently, Senanga offers a marvellous view of the floodplains.

Petrol and groceries are available, but motor spares and mechanical help are likely to be basic. Three alternatives for accommodation exist. There is the usual and typical government rest house. The Barotse Fishing Safari Lodge is private and must be booked through Barotse Fishing Safaris in Lusaka. It is superbly sited right on the water's edge. Next door is the best option for casual travellers, the Senanga Safari

Lodge, which has a wonderful view and offers a range of accommodation to suit most budgets in clean, well serviced and private rondavels set in a pleasant garden. Alas, a satellite dish placed in the middle of the lawn with all the reverence a Catholic mission might accord a statue of the Madonna, intrudes on the view almost as much as does the noise it produces from the set in the bar. Still, the terrace is the place to meet in Barotseland and there is a pleasant atmosphere. The lodge has boats for hire and some fishing tackle.

The Ngonye Falls

These falls at Sioma are second only to the Victoria Falls in magnitude and splendour. Although the falls are not particularly high, the sheer volume of water that thunders over the dyke is spectacular. Many visitors to the falls are misled into thinking that the view from the village of Sioma represents the sum total of the experience. In fact to see the falls properly it is necessary to cross the river by proceeding about 2 km downstream, where there is a dugout canoe that ferries people to and from the opposite bank. Precise directions are difficult, so ask around. A vehicle track leaves the road for a few hundred metres to end above a small dune-sided gorge. It is advisable to ask a local or scout from the NPWS office at Sioma to guide you. If you insist on going alone: having crossed the Zambezi by means of this canoe there is a path that ascends a sand dune and then forks. Take the left fork upstream and follow this footpath for about 2 km. It is reasonably clear. Eventually the roar of water will tell that you are getting close. The footpath emerges from the woodland at a wide and shallow stream of water running over a small fall to your left. Other than in March/April this stream should be quite safe (there are no crocodiles here), so ford it. From here the way to the falls is fairly obvious. Another fall and the buildings of Sioma can be seen on the opposite bank behind, but keep right and after crossing another small stream and some rocks you will arrive at the main fall, which sweeps away from under your feet in a great arcing deluge of foaming water. June or July are the best seasons to see the falls. In the months before them the water is so high that it rushes right over the falls and by the end of the dry season the falls lose a lot of their grandeur. A new lodge on the Zambezi downstream from the falls offers boat excursions to see them and is even planning white-water rafting through local rapids. See chapter 13.

SIOMA NATIONAL PARK

Location: This harsh wilderness without roads, landmarks or even much water is located in the south-western corner of Zambia between the Zambezi and the borders with Angola and Namibia.

How to get there: Only one safari company operates in this park at the moment, but there are no permanent facilities. The park is reached from the Sesheke/Katima Mulilo-Mongu road (see Route 5). Prospective visitors should be well equipped, preferably with two vehicles, and four-wheel-drive is essential. Petrol is only available at Sesheke or across the border at Katima Mulilo in Namibia and at Senanga. The park has no roads other than one around the fringes of the park connecting the main road at Kalabolelwa (35 km north of Katima Mulilo) via Ngwezi Pools with the Quando River. Finding this road is a mission in itself and you will save yourself no end of trouble by reporting to the NPWS office at Sioma opposite the Ngonye Falls and requesting the services of a guide. Even then you are dealing with a huge intractable wilderness in which you may need several days to find the harassed wildlife. A word of caution: the authors know from experience that it may be very hazardous indeed to attempt to leave existing tracks without the services of an experienced scout.

What to see: This is Kalahari sandveld country with dry miombo or acacia and terminalia woodland. There are areas of Zambezi teak forest and a few open grassy dambos around pans or pools. The eastern side of the reserve around Ngwezi Pools is quite populated. Deep in the thickets and undisturbed dambos this reserve is said to still harbour considerable herds of game, including as many as 3 000 elephants. Alas, poaching remains rife and animals, particularly elephants, are shy.

However, you are likely to see sable, roan and tsessebe, and this is the only place in Zambia outside the South Luangwa where there are giraffe. There's plenty of evidence of elephant but it will take patience and luck to find them. It is certainly lion country.

Where to stay: There is no infrastructure in the park at all. Try to head for Malombe, Kasaye or Kalau waterholes on the western side of the park for the greatest likelihood of finding game. For this a guide is essential.

An alternative to trying to get too deep into the park itself might be to take the track from Kalabolelwa to Ngwezi Pools and then turn right and head back on quite good track along the northern boundary of the park towards Sioma. If attempting this in the reverse, the road is fairly clear a few kilometres south of Sioma, but you are advised to seek more explicit directions from the wildlife officer in charge at the NPWS office in Sioma. This should still only be attempted by experienced bush travellers in reliable four-wheel-drive vehicles. Even though there are occasional villages, there's some chance of seeing game – perhaps even elephant – and it certainly gives you a taste of an Africa little changed for centuries. The journey can easily be accomplished in two days. In time this park will be opened up. Plans are afoot to make better roads into it. But until then it is a wild corner suitable only for hardy and experienced bush travellers.

LIUWA PLAIN NATIONAL PARK

Location: Between the Zambezi and Angola north of Kalabo.

How to get there: This is a very difficult park to access and it is recommended that use is made of Robin Pope Safaris – the only company operating in the park at the moment. However, permission for private parties can be obtained from the NPWS offices at Chilanga or the local NPWS HQ at Kalabo. But be warned, although the terrain in the park itself makes for relatively easy driving, getting across the Zambezi and as far as Kalabo is another matter altogether. Four options exist. The post boat which can carry one vehicle runs between Mongu and Kalabo when the water is high enough between April and June. When the water is low there are two ferry options, one directly out of Mongu at Sandaula and one at Libonda. The roads to and from these ferries are both difficult, even hazardous. When the water is too low for the post boat but still too high for these ferries, the only remaining option is to cross the river below Senangu at Sitoti and proceed north to Kalabo. But treat this as a last resort as the road is terribly sandy. Big four-wheel-drives may do the trip in a day, but it took the authors in a Land Rover two full days of low-range driving to complete the 180 km journey. And remember there is no fuel in Kalabo, so all fuel requirements must be carried on board and heavy sands will dramatically increase consumption. In Kalabo the NPWS officer in charge will supply a guide, who will be absolutely essential to navigation in the park.

It will then be necessary to commandeer the pontoon to cross the Luwinginga River. It is likely that the pontoon rope will have disappeared; enquire at the municipal offices. You will then have to row the rope across the river, before pulling your vehicle across on the pontoon.

Once across the river it is a distance of some 30 km to the park, although there is no formal gate.

What to see: The park is unique in Zambia, consisting of a huge, flat, grassy plain fringed with low broad-leafed woodland. Crossing the middle of the plain and seeing nothing but a sea of waving grass stretching to the furthest horizon all round you is a spectacular experience. Large, perennial herds of zebra and tsessebe and vast herds of migratory wildebeest are the main game. The most numerous predators are wild dogs and hyaena but lions are often seen. Other species include roan and a prolific number of oribi. Buffalo and red lechwe occur right in the northern corner of the park near the Luambimba River.

Birdlife is excellent, particularly around waterholes and pans.

Where to stay: There are no facilities whatsoever and there is no potable water other than a spring near Minde game scout village.

Final words of caution: Remember all fuel and water will have to be carried on board. Other than the tracks to Minde and Luula camps there are no roads to speak of. Do take a guide. Don't even think of venturing off the track without a compass. The park is still heavily poached both by Zambians and Angolans who may be heavily armed. Get advice on the security situation beforehand. Neighbouring Angola is close by with no border to speak of. If, in spite of all the above, you still want to see this barely travelled area, we vouch for its unique and delicate beauty and ask that special care be taken to preserve an environment so fragile that even vehicle tracks can cause irreparable damage.

WEST LUNGA NATIONAL PARK

Location: Between the West Lunga and Kabompo rivers.

How to get there: This park is undeveloped and not easily accessible at the moment. However the Kabompo River at the park boundary can be accessed at Jivundu some 40 km north of Kabompo on the Kabompo-Solwezi road. From Lusaka proceed either to Mumbwa and then on to Kasempa via the Lubungu ferry, a route that passes through wilderness in the Lunga-Luswishi Game Management Area. Or go round through the Copperbelt and Solwezi turning off to Kabompo just after Mutanda. The latter is a better road but longer.

The turnoff to Jivundu has a signpost clearly visible from the Solwezi side, but if coming from Kabompo look out carefully for it, the left turn doubles back sharply. At the moment the pontoon is broken and the river cannot be crossed to get into the park itself. Alternatively a scout from the Solwezi NPWS office may be persuaded to guide visitors in from the north, a dubious route untried by the authors. Whichever route is chosen, a four-wheel-drive vehicle will ultimately be essential.

What to see: Magnificently tall forests of several types are interspersed with grassy dambos and perennial papyrus swamps along the rivers. Poorly managed in recent years, the park has lost most of its once considerable wildlife to poaching. However it is said to still harbour a fair quantity of elephant and buffalo and scouts report hearing lions.

There are sable and certainly puku, sitatunga and Defassa waterbuck. Unusual animals to look out for are blue and yellow-backed duiker and a number of the lesser carnivores. The village of Jivundu is dreary but a scout will guide visitors to the river's edge a short distance away, where one can camp in beautiful solitude under big riverine trees and palms. Although there's little likelihood of seeing all the species listed above there are plenty of puku and bushbuck and great birdlife. A unique albino puku is the toast of the village. There are hippos but they are shy. Beware of crocodiles which, according to a local missionary, have cottoned onto human beings as an attractive prey species.

An interesting adjunct to the history of the park is found in the legendary exploits of a former warden of the park, one Mushala, who in the 1970s rebelled against the former regime, went to Angola for training in guerrilla warfare and returned to establish a Robin Hood-like fief in the West Lunga forests, from which he sallied forth at intervals to rob banks and harass government agencies before retreating apparently to distribute the spoils to local villagers. It says something of the West Lunga that it took the Zambian army 10 years to hunt down and finally shoot him. It is said by some that he was responsible for the radical decline of game, but by others that blame for that destruction lies with the government forces who hunted him; and that in fact Mushala should be thanked for the fact that game remains at all.

Where to stay: At the time of writing there were no facilities whatever, so visitors should ask at Jivundu for directions to a suitable campsite.

ROUTES (Western Region)
Route 5: Livingstone to Mongu via Sesheke
Total distance: 525 km. Time: Approximately 10 hours.
Potholed tar and sand. Four-wheel-drive preferable.
Recommended stops: Ngonye Falls. Senanga.

Petrol at Sesheke/Katima Mulilo, Senanga.

From Livingstone the gateway to western province is Nakatindi Road, leading to Kazungula about 60 km away on a reasonable tar road. Although seldom visible, the Zambezi is always evident from its shallow valley to the left of the road. From Kazungula there are two options; either to proceed straight ahead on the main road or to cross the river and go via Botswana and Namibia.

The first option through Mambova to Sesheke may seem the obvious choice, but it is an appalling road. The tar has collapsed and broken up to such an extent that it is no exaggeration to say there are more holes than even surface.

The 100-odd km will take several bone-crushing hours. Then at Sesheke take the first major road to the left which leads down to the ferry on which it is necessary to cross the Zambezi at a cost of US $25. If you have a sturdy vehicle you may opt for this rather than the fatiguing series of six border procedures needed on the other route. Sesheke itself was once the capital of the Lozi kingdom and near here the earliest traces of Bantu occupation in Zambia have been found, but of this illustrious history nothing remains to be seen and there is little to detain travellers on either bank of the river at this point.

The advantages of going through Botswana and Namibia are that Kasane and Katima Mulilo are well supplied, have reliable petrol and diesel and a choice of places to stay that vastly outclass anything on the other side of the river. The roads are gravel, but well maintained. At Kazungula after going through border procedures cross the river by ferry. Do check that you have a multiple entry visa for Zambia otherwise you will have to pay for another one on re-entry. Alternatively negotiate with the border officials for a temporary exit permit. From Kasane proceed for 64 km through the Chobe National Park to Ngoma Bridge, the Namibian border. The stretch through Namibia to Katima Mulilo is 63 km long and a good dirt road in the dry season, but be very careful in the wet when it can be slippery. Katima Mulilo in Namibia is a slightly wild town but all basic supplies and petrol are available there. The village of Katima Mulilo in Zambia has nothing besides a government rest house of dubious respectability.

Whichever of the above options one has taken, the road north from here proceeds on the west bank of the Zambezi. It is 140 km to the village of Sioma at the Ngonye Falls along a reasonable gravel road that does get sandy in a few patches. Off to the west lies the Sioma

National Park, which is described earlier in this chapter. The river is almost always visible from the road and the area is continuously populated. The practice of *chitemene* agriculture has cleared much of the vegetation close to the road, but travellers will notice that certain trees have been exempted from this destruction. This is because they belong to species specially protected under Lozi traditional law for their medicinal or food value or just because they provide good shade. At Kalabolelwa there is often an NPWS picket. The village of Sioma is small and only the brick walls and tin roofs of the National Parks and Wildlife Service offices a few hundred metres off to the right indicate that you have reached it. There is no petrol and no shops to speak of. But do stop over and go and look at the Ngonye Falls (see p. 97). The NPWS have a basic campsite.

As described earlier in this chapter, the Ngonye Falls mark the first of the basalt dykes that hold back the sands and waters of the Barotse floodplains. As the road approaches Sitoti it leaves the bush behind. At Sitoti turn down to the river. The road straight ahead is the track to Kalabo. A short description of the journey further north on this side of the river is given at the end of this route.

The ferry at Sitoti will again cost foreign visitors the astronomical sum of US $25 or R60. Travellers dismayed by this expense need look no further than 100 m downstream for an explanation – here lies the mangled remains of the old ferry, which was bombed – by the South Africans during the Namibian war.

Normally the Sitoti ferry simply crosses the river directly but at the height of the annual flooding in April, when the road on the other side may be under water, it is forced to travel 17 km upstream to Senanga which is very time-consuming and will cause considerable delays.

Normally, however, the road to Senanga is dry and simply potholed. For the first time northbound travellers really become aware of the floodplains which stretch away on all sides. There is petrol and accommodation in Senanga. From Senanga to Mongu there is a good tar road 116 km long.

Maps of Zambia indicate a direct road from Sitoti to Kalabo on the west bank of the river, but nobody in their right mind will willingly choose to negotiate it when they can go to Mongu and take a ferry back across the river from there.

However, occasionally when the water is too high for normal ferries yet too low for the post boat, it is necessary for traffic to Kalabo to use this route. The entire 180 km is deep Kalahari sand and in most seasons it will require a lot of low-range four-wheel-drive to plough through. The road proceeds through thick miombo woodland punctuated by villages.

Alternatively, a route that is more fun but no less arduous can be found along the very edge of the floodplain. This is really no more than a sled track that hops and winds through a continuous chain of villages. Skilled driving is called for so as not to run down dogs, chickens, children or the old and infirm. In the latter half of the dry season it is possible to find a track that traverses the middle of the floodplain itself, which will make for much easier driving. But it is difficult to find. To get onto the floodplain turn right at the first big tree after Sinungu. Note that many maps indicate a ferry across the Southern Lueti. In fact a dyke and bridge have been built. This side of the Zambezi is remote and little travelled, so visitors should be self-sufficient and well prepared. There is no petrol to be had anywhere, so carry enough for at least 500 km of low-range driving. There is no potable water until Kalabo.

However, for those willing to deal with the driving slog the floodplain is an inspiring experience. In the evenings when the cattle have been kraaled and the fish hung up to dry, the sound of cowhide drums and xylophones gently fills the vast, gathering darkness with a rhythm that seems to reverberate right from the timeless heartbeat of the continent itself.

Route 6: Lusaka to Mongu

Total distance: 581 km. Time: 6 hours.
Tar with minor potholes.
Recommended stopover: Kafue National Park.
Petrol at Mumbwa and Kaoma.

Leave Lusaka on the Mumbwa road to the Kafue National Park as described in Route 2. Mumbwa itself lies a few kilometres north of the road 150 km from Lusaka. Petrol and basic supplies are available there. After the first picket at Nalusanga the Kafue National Park lies on the north side of the road until you cross the magnificent Kafue River. Try to drive this section in the early morning when the possibility of seeing game en route is good. This region has some magnificent deciduous forests. Sadly, outside the park they are being harvested at an alarming rate, especially for the much sought after "Rhodesian teak", *Baikiaea plurijuga*, and mukwa tree, *Pterocarpus angolensis*. Kaoma is 78 km from the west gate of the national park. Again the town lies a little north of the road but there is a petrol station on the road. Travellers wishing to turn towards Lukulu and North-western Province note that the turnoff is a distinct gravel road heading north-west immediately beyond the second river crossing after the fuel station. Some 15 minutes down that road it forks where you should bear right.

Those proceeding to Mongu just carry on straight down the tar road for 186 km.

Route 7: From Mongu north to the source of the Zambezi via Lukulu, Chavuma, Zambezi, Kabompo and Mwinilunga

Time: 2 or 3 days.

Sandy tracks for which four-wheel-drive is advisable.

Petrol is scarce. The only fuel station is in Mwinilunga, but fuel can sometimes be bought at a price from IRDP depots or missions in other towns.

The best road to Lukulu is the one from Kaoma mentioned in Route 6. In the dry season it is possible to proceed straight north from Mongu by taking the road across the floodplain to Lealui and then heading north past the Libonda ferry. This way is extremely sandy and although more picturesque it will be slow going. Between Libonda and Lukulu is the camp of Barotse Fishing Safaris, accommodation at which is best booked in advance. Lukulu itself is not particularly interesting although the view from the Sancta Maria Mission over the Zambezi toward the Liuwa Plains is quite magnificent.

From Lukulu the road turns eastwards and improves a little for the 72 km to the Watopa ferry. Be sure to turn down to the ferry rather than proceeding straight on through the village, where the road becomes a narrow track back to Kaoma. The Watopa ferry is manually operated and like all pontoons of this size gives free passage across the river – in this case the Kabompo, which is a major tributary of the Zambezi.

It is possible to skip Lukulu and proceed directly to the Watopa Ferry from Kaoma by turning right about 102 km along the Lukulu road. The road is boldly signposted as the M8, but don't be deceived; it is a tiny, sandy track that winds its way for miles through uninhabited bush and some dense forests.

If you have time and preferably a four-wheel-drive, it is a delightful track to take. Eventually it becomes even narrower as it reaches a more populated region and then a right turn marks the pontoon. To proceed straight would, as described above, take you the 72 km to Lukulu. From the Watopa Ferry it is 21 km to the main Kabompo-Zambezi road, the much touted M8. Turn left if heading for Zambezi and Chavuma. The road has recently been upgraded and is one of the best gravel roads in the country. It is a beautiful drive, passing through mile after mile of seemingly untouched forests. The town of Zambezi, 75 km away, has a real central African feel about it with its mission church, muddy streets and low-slung buildings under a green canopy of trees. The only place to stay is the sleazy Zambezi Motel which won't win any prizes – architectural or otherwise – but does have an excellent view of the Zambezi River. Don't stop. Head north out of town and it is 82 km to Chavuma. Worth seeing en route is the suspension bridge over the Zambezi to the Capuchin mission at Chinyingi. Look out for an un-signposted but fairly obvious track branching to the west about 1,5 km after the bridge over the Mkondo River. If you miss this turn there is another, signposted to the Chinyingi mission a few kilometres further on. The reason to see this remarkable structure, built by the missionaries after the old ferry capsized, drowning several of their colleagues, is that it is the first of only four bridges across the entire length of the river. Victoria Falls, Chirundu and Tete are the other three. Walking over it is an experience and it makes for spectacular photographs at sunset.

The only reasons to see Chavuma are that it is very close to where the Zambezi comes out of Angola, the river runs over the Chavuma Falls (which are spectacularly disappointing at all times other than the flood season) and it is the site of one of the oldest missions in the region. The Brethren Mission is located on a hill and has a citadel-like command over the entire area.

If planning to spend a night here enquire at the mission about their campsite. It is reached by taking the road to the erstwhile pontoon immediately below the falls and then proceeding along a right fork past the school. Follow this sandy track for about 3 km. The campsite is used as a place of seclusion by the mission and has a few ramshackle buildings with some rooms of monastic appearance. The site above a broad sandbank is pleasant. Plans are afoot to provide another campsite downstream for campers only.

A pleasant walk can be taken from the west bank of the river upstream to another waterfall on the Kashiji River. Take the *mokoro* ferry across the river directly west of the mission. There is a fairly obvious path, but ask locals for directions. At the falls there is a beautiful clear pool. Beware of crocodiles. Because Chavuma is very near the Angolan border, local police and military are sticky about security and if planning any such local excursions it is advisable to inform them of your intentions beforehand.

To proceed north from here it is necessary to go back through Zambezi to Kabompo, a distance of 153 km. The gravel road is excellent most of the way. Spread out as it is under the trees on the south-east side of the road, it would be easy to pass by Kabompo without noticing it. While driving on these north-western roads travellers may notice curious structures made of bark high up in some of the trees. They are beehives and the best reason to stop in Kabompo is to visit the honey factory and buy some of this absolutely delicious forest honey. (It is also available in some Lusaka shops.) Anyone will be able to direct you there. If not, ask for the IRDP depot. It is right next door. Petrol can also be bought from the honey factory but note that they are closed on weekends. In addition to the above Kabompo has a Catholic and a CMML mission. There is a government rest house that is pleasantly located but rather disreputable.

If looking for somewhere in the region to spend the night, rather ask directions to where you can camp on the Kabompo River or proceed up to Jivundu about 70 km away, where the river marks the border of the West Lunga National Park (see p 100). A local politician and businessman is planning a campsite near the town.

From Kabompo there are two options for proceeding north.

Either carry straight on up the main road for 327 km to the Solwezi-Mwinilunga road, from where it is 242 km to Mwinilunga. It is a good road through woodland country and you may even be lucky enough to see elephants crossing it. Or take the back road to Mwinilunga which turns north at Loloma. This road is suitable for four-wheel-drive vehicles only. Heading north from Kabompo one crosses a small clear stream after about 25 km. Shortly afterwards turn left and double back to Muzama Woodcrafts (where incidentally some very good furniture is made from local timber). Proceed past the workshop and bear right past Loloma Primary School. There are some thatch cottages on the left; bear right and keep right where the road forks along the most used track until it joins what was obviously the original route from Manyinga.

From there you cannot go wrong and the track proceeds for 218 km more or less straight north through sporadic villages and large tracts of truly magnificent forest. The road is rather sandy in places and sometimes, especially through Lusongwa village, it is rutted and bumpy. Set aside at least 7 hours for this trip. The track eventually comes out just west of the bridge over the West Lunga River, immediately before Mwinilunga.

In Mwinilunga there are both a council and government rest house. The latter is quieter and more hygienic than the former. Petrol and diesel are usually available. For mechanical problems ask for the mechanic at the ZESCO depot.

The main road heads straight west out of town where after a few kilometres it reverts to a dirt track. The turnoff to the source of the Zambezi is about 50 km away and marked by a faded blue sign. The road to Kalene Hill and Sakeji is 67 km from Mwinilunga.

Route 8: Copperbelt to Mwinilunga

Distance: 450 km. Time: 5 hours.
Reasonably good tar road.
Petrol at Solwezi.

Visitors wishing to see the north-western corner of Zambia and the source of the Zambezi, but not able to take the four-wheel-drive route described earlier, can get there in a normal car by proceeding through the Copperbelt. From Chingola it is 173 km to Solwezi. The road is straightforward and the only warning that need be given, is that this is the one road in Zambia where it is inadvisable to pick up passengers or leave your vehicle unattended. The area is plagued by bandits from Zaïre who hijack vehicles and take them back over the nearby border.

About 60 km from Chingola is the turnoff on the right-hand side to Chimfunshi Farms and Wildlife Orphanage, which has become famous as a refuge for chimpanzees. Dave and Sheila Siddle welcome visitors, but have their hands full coping with an ambitious programme to re-introduce these abused primates to the wild.

Solwezi is a bustling town. There is petrol, there are banks and shops for basic supplies and the Changa Changa Hotel is a reasonable establishment with decent en-suite facilities.

From Solwezi the road turns south for about 35 km to meet the Kabompo road at Mwelemu. Here there is usually a NPWS picket with a boom across the road. Then it swings west again and it is 240 km to Mwinilunga. For the most part the area is densely populated with a string of villages flanking the road. There is little to stop for, but about 72 km before Mwinilunga a road heads south and by following it for 13 km and then turning right onto a very poor track for another 2 km you can get to the Nyambwezu Falls. They are not spectacular, but there is a rock shelter just the other side of the lip of the falls which has prehistoric engravings of curious lines and dots.

One would imagine that finding the source of the Zambezi requires a Rider Haggard-like expedition through mysterious jungly mountains. Actually there are no mountains to speak of and it couldn't be easier to find. You can reach it by driving straight out of Mwinilunga, westwards for about 50 km. Shortly after leaving town the tar ends and the road narrows into a lane running for miles through the trees. A faded blue sign on the right-hand side of the road marks the entry to the heritage site. Having turned and signed in, proceed for about 4 km down the access road until it ends at an independence monument.

There is a clear footpath down the hill into a patch of "rainforest". Do apply mosquito repellent liberally beforehand as the valley is full of the little pests. The path ends at a delightful, clear rivulet of water that appears to emanate from the bowl of a fallen tree. In fact the real source is a little higher up and can be found by taking a small track upstream some 10 m back from where the main path ends.

This little path winds between the trees and occasionally the tiny stream is visible burrowing through the mossy roots underfoot. Eventually you come upon a clear pool of water and it is incredibly moving to watch it drain over the leaf-strewn ground on its first passage to becoming that mighty, mighty river. Incidentally, it is amazing to think that the source of that other huge African waterway, the Zaïre or Congo River, is only a few kilometres away. There is a campsite at the monument with a pit latrine.

For those interested in the history of the territory it is worth visiting Kalene Hill and Sakeji where the descendants of the pioneer missionary, Dr Walter Fisher, live at Hillwood Farm. A part of the farm has been set aside for game and there are plans to establish a small self-catering lodge and camping facility. This is an ideal stepping-stone for Kalene Hill. However, it is a private farm and visitors should enquire at the farm office before proceeding.

Kalene Hill is best visited in the company of Joan Hoyt, who can extract from the otherwise dull ruins a fascinating and lively story of the early days at the mission. A pamphlet is available for unaccompanied visitors. To get to the hill turn left at the T-junction if coming from Mwinilunga. (The road on the right goes to the farm and Sakeji school, so if coming from there simply go past the Mwinilunga road.) After crossing a bridge en route to Mwininyilamba keep right past the road camp and through a village and then bear left at the next fork (the right fork goes to the present mission and is the way to go to see the Zambezi before it runs into Angola). About 2 km further on the road bisects a large anthill at the end of a mud-brick village. Look for a track bearing right. It is about 1,5 km from there to the hill, the last part of which is very stony and probably requires a four-wheel-drive. The ruins of the old mission have all but disappeared and it is hard to imagine the once thriving community from the rocky outcrop, but the view out over Angola and Zaïre is terrific.

The mission on Kalene Hill was founded in 1905 by Walter Fisher, a "Brethren" doctor who had followed Fred Arnot to Africa in 1889 and practised and preached from missions in the Angolan hinterland. Arnot was married to Fisher's elder sister. The name Kalene Hill is derived from that of Ikalenje, a Lunda chieftain in the region. It was wild and primitive country and the story of these early missionaries is one of striking faith and endurance in the face of persistent hardship. It is told in two books: *Ndotulu – The life stories of Walter and Anna Fisher* by W Singleton Fisher and Julyan Hoyt, and *Nswana – The Heir*, by Monica Fisher. The former is out of print but the latter was published fairly recently and can be found in bookshops in Lusaka. A little way down the north-western side of the hill on the path from the new mission are the graves of Walter and Anna Fisher. Their graves look out over a vast intractable wilderness still lost in a hazy tropical ether where so much and yet so little has changed since their arrival a century ago.

9 THE COPPERBELT

Between 600 and 1 000 million years ago the landmass of what is now central Africa underwent an oceanic invasion from the west. Over aeons water erosion leached gravels and clay, and dissolved mineral salts from the highlands. And in the shallow lagoons and estuaries of that primordial soup primitive plant and animal matter produced sulphurated oxygen which in turn precipitated sulphides of copper as well as cobalt, nickel and iron. Then the oceans advanced; huge sediments were laid down. The globe cooled and glaciers pushed enormous boulders down from the north. In the chilly seas primitive life flourished.

When the climate warmed more sediments were deposited and then the landmass was subjected to terrific tectonic uplift and folding. 250 million years ago a second ice age occurred, after which the land became a dry and waterless desert. Another massive tectonic shift lifted this part of the continent a thousand metres. When streams broke through they stained the rocks with green. From about the 4th century Bantu populations long settled in the area began to exploit the traces of copper that this revealed.

Then in 1902 a prospector, William Collier, was hunting (or so it is said) along the Luanshya River, when he shot a roan antelope bull in an open dambo and it fell on a green-stained rock. And so was unleashed a process that disembowelled in a century a geomorphology wrought over a billion years. The Copperbelt, in an area 50 km wide and just twice as long, became one of the greatest copper-producing areas of the world; at one time churning out as much as 800 000 tons of copper a year. The decline of world copper prices and depletion of resources have somewhat jaded the once-thriving industry.

In truth the Copperbelt is of limited tourist interest to anyone not fascinated by mining. It is densely populated and environmentally ravaged but it has for a long time been the commercial and industrial centre of the country. Kitwe considers itself the hub of the Copperbelt, but Ndola is the biggest and most important city.

NDOLA

Ndola is really more of a large spread-out town than a city, but it is the second biggest city after the capital. Its origins were as a railhead

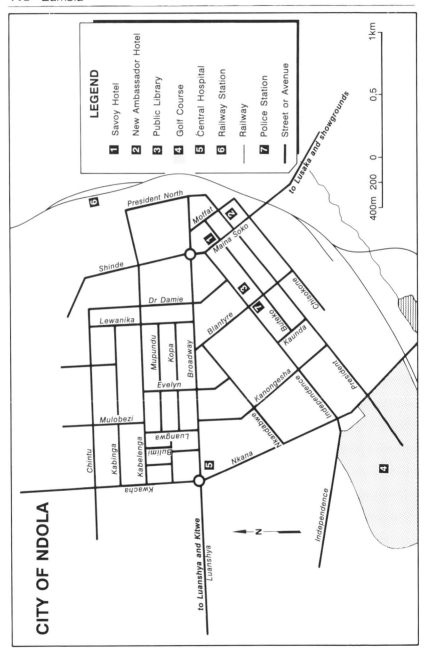

CITY OF NDOLA

LEGEND

1 Savoy Hotel
2 New Ambassador Hotel
3 Public Library
4 Golf Course
5 Central Hospital
6 Railway Station
— Railway
7 Police Station
— Street or Avenue

to Lusaka and showgrounds

to Luanshya and Kitwe

President North

Moffat

Maina Soko

Chisokone

Shinde

Dr Damie

Lewanika

Blantyre

Butako

Kaunda

Mupundu

Kopa

Broadway

Evelyn

Kanongesha

Independence

President

Mulobezi

Luangwa

Bulimi

Nkandabwe

Nkana

Chintu

Kabinga

Kabelenga

Kwacha

Independence

Luanshya

and distribution centre. The Ndola boma was established in 1904. With the growth of secondary industries around the copper mines, rapid and extensive development has turned it into the commercial and industrial hub of the country. But a typical industrial city it is not, being a rather pleasant town with bustling, colourful President Avenue contrasting with the broad and leafy expanses of Independence Avenue and Broadway Road.

Access

By air: There are daily flights from Lusaka but no direct international flights, although Zambian Airways is considering introducing a flight from Johannesburg via Livingstone to Ndola.

By bus: The bus terminus is in Chimwemwe Avenue, just a short walk from the city centre. Some buses seem to arrive and depart behind the Savoy Hotel off Main Soko Road.

By rail: Two passenger trains operate between Livingstone and the Copperbelt via Lusaka. The railway station is at the extreme north end of President Avenue. To get to the city centre proceed down President Avenue until it intersects with Broadway Road then turn up Broadway for two blocks and turn right into Moffet. Or go straight down President as far as Main Soko Road.

By car: Ndola is 320 km north of Lusaka on the main road, passing straight through Kabwe and Kapiri Mposhi. One can enter Ndola two ways, from Lusaka straight down Main Soko Road or from Kitwe and Luanshya down Luanshya Road (which becomes Broadway Road).

Tourist information

Most banks and travel agencies are located in Buteko Avenue near the Savoy Hotel. President Avenue is the main commercial street. The Central Hospital is on the corner of Nkana and Broadway roads. Vehicle repairs and parts are best sought in Chisokone Avenue, one down and parallel to President Avenue.

Accommodation

There are really only three alternatives in Ndola. The Savoy in Buteko Avenue is the most exclusive and very centrally located with a quietly cosmopolitan atmosphere. The New Ambassador in President Avenue is at the other end of the market but also very central and then there is the Mukuba Hotel, which is in the Trade Fair grounds and so a little out of town but nevertheless very pleasant. Take Main Soko Road out under the railway line and round to the industrial area, then look for a signposted turn to the right and follow the signs.

KITWE

With the start of mining in the 1920s and further prospecting, very rich ore deposits were found close to the Kafue River and what became the Nkana Mine was first sunk in 1928. In 1935 a township was laid out along the Kitwe stream for the benefit of traders attracted to the mining operations. By a curious proclamation the colonial government decreed that no other township could be established within a ten-mile radius and so Kitwe became, as it still asserts itself today, the hub of the Copperbelt. Rivalling Ndola in size, it is physically not an unpleasant town although it has little to offer tourists besides essential services.

Access

By air: Kitwe has a reasonable airport at South Downs, 10 km west of the city, but flights from Lusaka land at Ndola Airport, 60 km away.

By rail: The Zambian railways passenger service from Livingstone and Lusaka operates as far as Kitwe. The railway station is very close to the city centre, off Oxford Road.

By bus: The intercity bus station is in what is known as the second-class trading area.

By car: Kitwe is 58 km from Ndola. Those arriving from Ndola and the south will enter Kitwe on a dual carriageway, which becomes President Avenue. One block west is Independence Avenue, which from Oxford Road is the main thoroughfare through Kitwe and continues northwards to connect Kitwe with Chingola.

Tourist information

The city centre lies astride Independence and President avenues and most shopping and banking will be found here. The Civic Centre is on the west side of President Avenue and Kitwe Central Hospital lies just 2 km down Independence Avenue, immediately behind the fire station. Vehicle repairs are best sought along and west of Independence Avenue.

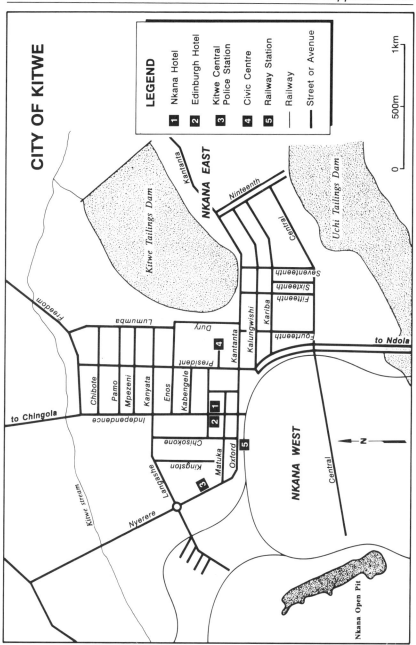

CITY OF KITWE

LEGEND

1 Nkana Hotel
2 Edinburgh Hotel
3 Kitwe Central Police Station
4 Civic Centre
5 Railway Station
— Railway
— Street or Avenue

Accommodation

There are really only two choices: the Nkana and Edinburgh hotels, which stand directly opposite each other on Independence Avenue two blocks north of Oxford Road. Both have assumed the status if, unfortunately, not the standards of international hotels and have corresponding prices. The Buchi Hotel is cheaper but about 6 km out of town. For backpackers there is a YMCA about 2 km further down on the left-hand side of Independence Avenue.

The other towns on the Copperbelt are Luanshya, south-west of Ndola, and then to the north-west of Kitwe: Mufulira, Chingola and Chililabombwe. Unless proceeding to Zaïre, the only one of these that visitors are likely to pass through is Chingola, which is a not unattractive town with trees and broad avenues but with nowhere pleasant to stay and nothing to detain travellers.

WHAT TO SEE AND DO IN THE COPPERBELT

For all its limited tourist potential the Copperbelt does have some places of interest which may be worth an excursion or detour on your way through.

The Copperbelt Museum on Buteko Avenue in Ndola has a display outlining the history of the Copperbelt, and examples of various ores as well as a small collection of stuffed animals so decrepit you might be forgiven for assuming they were representatives of extinct species. For better taxidermy see the bird collection in the foyer of the Mukuba Hotel.

Also in Ndola, in Makoli Avenue off Nkana Road 500 m south of President Avenue, stands an ancient *Afzelia quanzensis* or *Mupapa* tree. This is the Slave Tree and under its shade Swahili slave traders met and sold their captives. It is hard to imagine now, but the slave trade was only finally abolished in this part of the world with the establishment of the British colonial administration in the first decade of this century.

Another magnificent tree is the Chichele Mofu Tree – which you can't miss as it stands right in the middle of the dual carriageway between Ndola and Kitwe. According to local tradition it is an *Ngulu*, that is to say a house of spirits in which the spirit of a long-dead chief lives. The tree was declared a national monument in 1976 to commemorate World Forestry Day and at its foot stands a plaque with this well-known anonymous poem:

Ye who would pass by and raise your hand against me,
Harken ere you harm me.
I am the heat of your hearth on cold winter nights,
The friendly shade screening you from the summer sun;
And my fruits are refreshing draughts
Quenching your thirst as you journey on.
I am the beam that holds your house,
the board of your table,
the bed on which you lie
and the timber that builds your boat.
I am the handle of your hoe and the door of your
homestead, the wood of your cradle and the shell
of your coffin.
I am the gift of God and the friend of man.
Ye who passes by, listen to my prayer . . .
HARM ME NOT.

The spirit of that ancient chief must rest uneasily in those boughs as he surveys from the vantage of history the deforestation around him.

Also on the Ndola-Kitwe road is a signposted turnoff to the Dag Hammarskjöld memorial: a monument erected on the site where the former UN chief was killed in a mysterious air crash while on his way to intervene in the Katanga crisis in Zaïre in 1961. The memorial can also be reached by driving from Ndola on the Mufulira Road and then turning south-west about 10 km from Ndola. It is of limited tourist interest.

Where the Chingola-Chililabombwe road crosses the Kafue River is a recreational area known as the Hippo Pool. There are no longer hippos in this stretch of the river, but the area is scenic and a good birding spot. Some misgivings are expressed about its safety from petty crime.

The Collier monument in Luanshya is a 6-m copper obelisk marking the approximate spot where the prospector William Collier made the discovery related above that put the region on the map.

There are two interesting sunken lakes in the Copperbelt. Lake Kashiba is situated not far from St Anthony's Mission, about 70 km south-west of Mpongwe. It can also be reached by turning west down a secondary road some 32 km north of Kapiri Mposhi on the way to Ndola. There are basic camping facilities at the lake and it is a beautiful spot, well worth considering as a stopover for campers coming up from Lusaka en route to the north-west. There are no crocodiles so swimming is fine and there is said to be good birdwatching in the nearby forest. The lakes are apparently formed when schistose rock that makes up the surface collapses into sinkholes in the underlying limestone. Lake Kashiba is over 100 m deep. The National Monuments of Zambia booklet relates a legend surrounding a clan who lived in the area known as the Bena mbushi. Insulted in some inter-clan argument, the Bena mbushi all tied themselves to a very long rope. And so strung together they danced around their village before proceeding to the lake where link by link the great human chain threw themselves in and drowned. The very last person on the rope was a pregnant woman who was saved at the last minute and became the ancestor of the people today.

Another lake held in traditional reverence by the local people is Lake Chilengwa, which is smaller than Lake Kashiba and one of apparently several similar sunken lakes in the Ndola region. It is about 500 m across. It lies about 16 km south-east of Ndola, quite near the Zaïre border. To get there take the Ndola-Bwana Mkubwa Road. 5 km south of Ndola turn east and then take a left turn north just before Chiwala secondary school.

COPPERBELT ROUTE

Route 9: Lusaka to Ndola and Kitwe

Total distance: 358 km. All tar.
Recommended stops: Possibly divert via Lake Kashiba.
Petrol at Kabwe. Petrol at Kapiri is unreliable.

In Lusaka head straight north on Cairo Road, which beyond its north end circle becomes the Great North Road. The road is being rebuilt and you can expect good tar at first and then roadworks en route, with long and uncomfortable detours for the foreseeable future. Where roadworks have not yet commenced expect potholes. It's 68 km through the Chisamba farming block to Landless Corner, a large roadside store where you can get fresh produce. Some kilometres before Landless Corner you cannot miss the sign to Fringilla Farm which aside from having an excellent butchery, dairy and restaurant, offers accommodation in luxury chalets and camping facilities with hot running water. Fringilla is owned by the Woodley family, and more welcoming and hospitable people you could not hope to meet. In addition there is a workshop where vehicle repairs can be carried out at far more reasonable prices than can be found in town.

There is usually a roadblock at Landless Corner, then it's 70 km to Kabwe which is a pleasant, leafy town. From Kabwe it is 68 km to Kapiri Mposhi, railway junction for the famous Tazara line to Dar es Salaam and where the Great North Road splits to the Copperbelt and east Africa. It is a truckers' stop with a string of brightly painted bars and "nightspots". Colourful and fun to pass by, its highly questionable whether you'd want to spend the night.

The road through Kapiri is absolutely awful at the moment with huge crater-like potholes. Drive slowly and give way. About 30 km beyond Kapiri there's a turnoff left to Mpongwe and St Anthony's Mission which is the way to go to Lake Kashiba. Straight on it's about 67 km to where the road splits left for Kitwe. From Kapiri it's 115 km straight to Ndola. Between Ndola and Kitwe note the Chichele Mofu Tree mentioned previously and the turnoff to the Dag Hammarskjöld Memorial.

10 THE NORTHERN REGION

The rivers of this region are almost the only ones in the whole country that do not ultimately run into the Zambezi. Instead they drain from the watershed along the Great North Road into the Bangweulu Basin and then the Luapula River, which runs into Lake Mweru and eventually into the great Zaïre River itself. The Great North Road and the Tanzania-Zambia (Tazara) Railway are the region's lifeline to the rest of the country and for the most part follow the watershed between the Zambezi and Zaïre rivers. Today there is something awe-inspiring about driving up the Great North Road from Kapiri Mposhi, along the highway to east Africa, and seeing the hills roll away on either side of this continental divide between two of the greatest rivers on the planet. It is a large region with a relatively undeveloped tourist infrastructure, but in addition to several national parks and wilderness areas, northern Zambia has many scenic diversions from its principal highways. It is an area of high rainfall and large rivers with many beautiful waterfalls and, of course, great lakes that have found their way into the pages of history as the quests and sometimes the nemesis of European explorers. The region had a somewhat colourful colonial history. If the first naval battle of the First World War was fought on Lake Malawi, this region can claim the last surrender of that war, when General von Lettow Vorbeck gave himself up near Kasama. The Bemba are the predominant tribe in the region. The Lunda, who trace common origins with the Bemba, live in Luapula Province.

KASANKA NATIONAL PARK

This marvellous little park, centred on the Kapabi Swamp, is privately managed and a must-see for visitors to the area.

Location: Northern Zambia, south of the Bangweulu Basin.

How to get there: Kasanka is easily accessed by turning off the Great North Road (see Route 10) 39 km from Serenje onto the Mansa road. About 54,5 km from the turnoff the entrance to Kasanka is clearly marked on the left. Four-wheel-drive is not necessary, only advised for further excursions. Kasanka also has its own airstrip.

What to see: This little park, only 420 square kilometres in extent, is a gem. Once badly poached, it has been saved through the formation of the Kasanka Trust. It is the first privately managed national park in Zambia and a striking success story. The Trust represents the NPWS, private enterprise and the local population to ensure benefit to all from Kasanka's conservation. Although the park was almost devoid of wildlife in 1985, numbers of game have returned to its sanctuary – including elephant. But the park is best known as probably the world's best place to view sitatunga. These normally rare and very shy antelope can be seen by the dozen from a hide built high in a magnificent *Khaya nyasica,* or mululu, tree.

Kasanka has a variety of vegetation from dry evergreen forest to swamps and magnificent riverine trees. There is prolific birdlife with over 350 species recorded to date, including shoebills which are sometimes found in summer in the papyrus swamps at the southern end of the park. Mammal species seen include puku, bushbuck, Defassa waterbuck and reedbuck. There are Lichtenstein's hartebeest and sable, common duiker and Sharpe's grysbok, warthog and bushpig. Very occasionally yellow-backed duiker are seen. There are hippos and crocodiles, including some very large specimens of the latter.

Perhaps uniquely in Zambia the slender-snouted crocodile (*Crocodylus cataphractus*), which is a denizen of equatorial forests, has been recorded in Kasanka. Lions pass through but are not resident. Leopard and smaller carnivores are plentiful. In November and December Kasanka witnesses a quite extraordinary event: a million straw-coloured fruit bats emerge after sundown, filling the sky like a black cloud.

The park also offers good angling for tigerfish, bream and barbel.

Relatively close by are the memorial marking the spot where Livingstone died, the Kundalila Falls and the Nsalu Cave (see page 134). Kasanka makes a good springboard for an expedition into the Bangweulu Swamp.

When to go: Kasanka is open throughout the year. Game will be better in the dry season, birds in the summer. November and December is the time to see the remarkable bat colony.

Where to stay: Kasanka has three lodges. Wasa Lodge, which is the main camp, consists of small, charming rondavels with shared facilities set above a small lake, whereas the Luwombwa Fishing Lodge and Musande tented camp are both situated on the Luwombwa River. All are very reasonably priced and available on a self-catering basis or with full board if booked in advance. Campers can also use a fourth camp at Kankonto which has its own access at the 91-km mark on the Mansa road. Here basic cooking and washing facilities are provided, although visitors are expected to provide their own tents and bedding.

Kasanka will also organise trips to Shoebill Camp, their camp in the Bangweulu Swamp.

LAVUSHI MANDA NATIONAL PARK

Location: Directly east of Kasanka, between the Mansa Road and the Great North Road.

How to get there: This park is relatively easily accessed from the Great North Road. Turn west 46 km south of Mpika, or take the road to Chiundaponde from the Mansa road, 10 km from the Kasanka turnoff. This is also the road to the Livingstone Memorial and is signposted as such. After some 8 km the road forks left to the memorial. Keep right and then turn left about 12 km further on. From Chiundaponde the road goes directly to the park, with the entrance marked by a picket. This road eventually comes out on the Great North Road south of Mpika. In the dry season the road is relatively good most of the way, but washed out with big gullies in the region of the park.

What to see: The park runs from the Lavushi Hills on the Zambezi-Zaïre watershed down toward the Bangweulu Basin. Mixed broad-leafed woodland and open, grassy dambos make for very pretty terrain, but sadly the area has been poached of almost every living creature.

If you are lucky you may see a reedbuck or a grysbok. So the park is at most recommended as a scenic diversion en route northwards.

Where to stay: There are no formal facilities but with relatively easy access (although a four-wheel-drive or high clearance pick-up is recommended) there's many a scenic spot to choose to camp. The road that traverses the park is the only road.

ISANGANO NATIONAL PARK

Location: North-east of the Bangweulu swamp.

How to get there: Take the Great North Road to Mpika and then proceed towards Kasama for about 86 km. Turn left onto a secondary road which proceeds 43 km south-west to the village of Mbati which is on the Chambeshi River, the park boundary. The park has no internal road network. It is doubtful whether visitors can proceed across the river by vehicle at all.

What to see: The park comprises mostly well-watered floodplain, being part of the Bangweulu Basin. Once prolific game has, according to latest reports, virtually been poached out. Visitors are in fact better advised to go into the Bangweulu Game Management Area where the local game populations, including the unique black lechwe, are still plentiful (see below).

Where to stay: There are no facilities in this park whatsoever.

BANGWEULU GAME MANAGEMENT AREA

Bangweulu means "where the water meets the sky". This vast wetland is notorious as the morass in which Livingstone died under the delirious misconception that he had found the source of the Nile. The real lake is best seen from Samfya, but at the moment that offers little beyond a beach holiday in slightly seedy surroundings (see below). Much more interesting is the Bangweulu Game Management Area, which is probably the most exciting wildlife destination in northern Zambia and, like Lochinvar, a wetland listed as having international conservation importance under the RAMSAR convention.

Location: The Bangweulu Basin in its greatest extent lies between the Mansa road and the Great North Road, to the north of Kasanka and Lavushi Manda national parks.

How to get there: There is an airstrip at the WWF Wetlands camp at Chimbwi. By vehicle from the Great North Road turn to Mansa and then, just after the Kasanka turnoff or about 64 km from the GNR, a sign marks the way to the Livingstone Memorial. Turn right. At the next fork, where a sign points left to the memorial, proceed right then turn left at the next fork, to Chiundaponde. At Chiundaponde, instead of forking right to Lavushi Manda proceed straight to Ngungwa. The journey from the tar road is about 140 km and takes about six hours.

What to see: The Bangweulu is a magnificent wilderness but quite unlike any other in Zambia. It consists mainly of vast grassy flatlands and papyrus swamps interspersed with river channels and lakes. Because it is a game management area rather than a national park, the local population continue to support themselves by fishing. Wildlife is prolific. The black lechwe is endemic to these floodplains and can sometimes be seen in herds of up to 10 000 animals. In addition elephant, buffalo and tsessebe have adapted to life in the wetland and smaller antelope such as reedbuck, oribi and sitatunga are common.

Bangweulu has stunning birdlife with prolific numbers of waterfowl as well as Denham's bustard and that great central African dodo, for which these swamps are famous, the shoebill stork.

When to go: The Bangweulu is really only accessible by vehicle between May and December. However in the wet season boat transfers to Shoebill Island can be arranged.

Where to stay: Kasanka Wildlife Conservation Ltd run Shoebill Island camp for full catering or self-catering guests. Book in advance through Kasanka. Some of the safari companies based in the Luangwa Valley also run safaris to Bangweulu (see chapter 13).

LUSENGA PLAIN NATIONAL PARK

Location: Far northern Zambia, near Lake Mweru.

How to get there: Proceed to Kawambwa, either via Mporokoso or, preferably, by turning off the Great North Road to Mansa along a good tar road. At Mansa turn right and travel northwards for 168 km to Kawambwa. Enquire at the National Parks and Wildlife office in Kawambwa for a scout who can guide you into the park. Attempts to reach the park without such guidance are likely to end in failure.

What to see: This national park consists of a large grassy plain with outcrops of rock surrounded by miombo, evergreen and swamp forest and bordered on the east by the Kalungushwi River, which has three magnificent waterfalls. These waterfalls are better accessed from the Kawambwa-Mporokoso road (see page 134). The game has been slaughtered and that remaining will be extremely shy, but reedbuck, blue and yellow-backed duiker can be seen, and you may be lucky enough to spot buffalo. Deep in the forests outside the park and closer to Nchelenge a small herd of elephants apparently survives.

When to go: Between May and December.

Where to stay: There are no facilities whatsoever in the park and no roads. A guide will direct you to the best place to camp.

MWERU WANTIPA NATIONAL PARK

Location: Far northern Zambia between Lake Mweru and Lake Tanganyika.

How to get there: Take the Great North Road to Mpika and Kasama. From Kasama proceed to Mporokoso. Here the main road proceeds to

Lake Tanganyika, but continue through the town, westwards toward Chiengi where the main road from Mununga on Lake Mweru swings north. Turn right along this road which proceeds straight through the park with Lake Mweru Wantipa on your right. There are no other roads in the park.

What to see: This park used to have vast herds of elephant. Alas, poaching has wiped them out. There are still some buffalo herds and there are said to be a few herds of hartebeest, roan and sable, although evidence of these is slim. There may still be lions. Birdlife is excellent, especially along the shoreline.

When to go: May through to November or December.

Where to stay: There are no facilities. But during the dry season some of the large trees on the lakeshore and floodplain may be accessible for camping. The park is inaccessible during the rainy season.

SUMBU NATIONAL PARK

Location: Far northern Zambia, on the shores of Lake Tanganyika.

How to get there: There is a tar airstrip at Kasaba Bay to which (at the time of writing) Zambian Airways makes weekly flights and there are weekly charters by Roan Air. By road one proceeds up the Great North Road past Mpika to Kasama. From there take the Luwingu road and then 18,5 km from town turn right to Mporokoso, where you turn right and north towards Sumbu. At Sumbu there is a boom across the road and you will be directed right into the park. The road network in the park is limited to one bumpy and stony track to Nkamba Bay and Kasaba Bay. For this last section it is really necessary to have a four-wheel-drive or certainly a rugged vehicle. On some maps Sumbu National Park appears to be accessible from Mbala; note that this is definitely not possible as there is no way across the Lufubu River.

What to see: Despite the best efforts of insensitive development and poor management, this remarkable national park has not lost its appeal. The hillsides consist of dense, near-impenetrable thicket which is not particularly attractive in the dry season, but the lakeshore and flood-plains are more open for game viewing. Poaching has not yet entirely wiped out the elephants, some of which frequent the Kasaba Bay Lodge, and can be seen at closer quarters than anywhere else in the country. There are also buffalo, lion, leopard and a reasonable number of an-telope including roan, sable and waterbuck and a healthy population of puku. Hippos can be seen in the unusual setting of the lake which also harbours some of the largest crocodiles south of the equator. One look at "the poacher" hauling all 6 m of his vast reptilian bulk out of the lake at Kasaba Bay will convince visitors of the inadvisability of swimming.

The real reason people come to Kasaba Bay is to go game fishing for Goliath tigerfish and Nile perch. Boats can be hired from the lodges.

When to go: All year.

Where to stay: There are unfortunately no camping facilities in the national park and visitors will have to stay at either Kasaba Bay Lodge or Nkamba Bay Lodge, which despite proclaiming all the conveniences of modern hotels (unless they have run out of diesel or supplies, which is a not-infrequent occurrence) are overpriced.

The design and management of the lodges says a lot about Zambia's former seclusion from modern eco-tourism. (For details see chapter 12.) Game drives are probably better from Nkamba Bay although one can be guaranteed elephants, puku, hippos and crocodiles at Kasaba Bay.

Camping and slightly cheaper accommodation is available at Ndole Bay Lodge, which lies about 8 km west of Sumbu and hence well outside the boundaries of the national park.

SHIWA NGANDU and KAPISHYA HOT SPRINGS

Shortly before the First World War, a young British officer who had served on an Anglo-Belgian boundary commission to determine the border of the Congo decided to make his way back from Ndola to Dar es Salaam on foot. After crossing the Luapula River and the Bangweulu Swamp he found his way into a temperate region where he came upon a small but beautiful lake called Ishiba Ngandu, the Lake of the Royal Crocodiles. According to legend, at the beginning of this century the lake teemed with hippos and crocodiles, which terrorised the local inhabitants. So an army of 200 warriors was sent to destroy the marauding denizens of the lake. At the end of a day of great carnage the hippos and crocodiles had been slaughtered but of the brave 200 who had set forth in the morning, only a handful of warriors returned alive.

Whatever unquiet bones lay beneath its surface, young Stewart Gore Brown saw paradise reflected in the still waters and decided to make his home here. The war intervened and it was only in 1920, having survived the Battle of the Somme, that he could return. But return he did, with an army building manual and an extraordinary dream. In a wilderness barely explored and still teeming with game he imagined an English shire where the inhabitants would be drawn into working for his great estate and in return would be provided with houses, schools, clinics and a post office; in fact a utopian community over which he would preside from a seat befitting the grandeur of his ambitions.

Today, visitors who arrive at the gatehouse without being forewarned are likely to be quite bowled over, for that is exactly what he did. With bricks and timbers and roof tiles made on site and equipment and furniture (including a four-poster bed) brought from England to the railhead at Ndola and then 600 km across the Bangweulu Swamp (the Great North Road did not yet exist), he built the farm with all the amenities he had planned. And on the hillside overlooking it all he built a magnificent Tuscan manor house. He distilled essential oils from citrus and shipped out the high-value, low-bulk product on porters' heads to Ndola. A thriving industry developed and ran until after the Second World War when imported trees brought a virus that killed off all the citrus groves. He became a figurehead in Northern Rhodesian politics, was knighted by the Queen and further honoured by President Kaunda, of whom he became a great friend. When eventually he died, an octogenarian, in 1967, he had acquired the venerable and aristocratic status of Zambia's grand old man.

After three-quarters of a century the rain and sun have so beaten down upon the walls and roofs and ramparts of his vast estate that they look as if they are centuries old. At the bottom of the gardens where cypresses and deodars, eucalyptus and pine become entwined with a jungle of creepers and collapse into rampant forest, there is a sense of Africa and colonialism peacefully reconciled. Of all the extraordinary and sometimes bizarre legacies the colonial period bequeathed to the continent, this house is one of the most moving. To see Shiwa Ngandu and then turn one's gaze from the mouldering terraces to the distant shimmer of the lake is to stand in awe of the vision, the self-assuredness, the paternalism, the compassion and the sheer bloody mindedness that underscored the British colonial hand in Africa.

Today Stewart Gore Brown's grandchildren, the Harveys, have inherited the estate. It is still their family home. For many years they have run safaris from here down into the North Luangwa National Park (see chapter 11). At the same time they have run a small lodge at the Kapishya Hot Springs. Now they have decided to incorporate their home into the safari package and clients are invited to stay in the manor house and experience for themselves the lifestyle of a bygone era (see Shiwa Safaris, chapter 13).

Kapishya Hot Springs lies just 20 km from Shiwa Ngandu. Part of the great estate, it falls under the umbrella of Shiwa Safaris, but casual visitors are welcome to book into the lodge (it is best to book in advance) or camp close by. Zambia has many hot springs, but none to rival these. To bathe in the hot clear soda water of an unspoiled, sandy bottomed pool overhung with palm trees is wonderful; to do so at night with only the light of the moon or a storm lantern is a sensation that has to be experienced to be believed.

THE GREAT LAKES

Lake Bangweulu

This has been partly dealt with above. The open waters of the lake can be reached at Samfya, which is directly off the tar road between Serenje and Mansa. Plans have been made to establish a tourist resort here, but unless visitors have their own boats which could be launched here for fishing, there is little to attract anyone to Samfya. There are also plans for a luxury cruise boat which would ply the waters from here down the Luapula River.

Lake Mweru

Lake Mweru is right up in the north-western corner of the region and, together with the Luapula River which drains into it, forms part of the border with Zaïre. There is no established tourist infrastructure on Lake Mweru at all, and because its shores are very densely populated there is no particular destination for travellers to head for. As part of a comprehensive tour of the great lakes it is worth seeing, however, just for its great expanse. Fishermen are likely to find it particularly good for large bream, but it does not otherwise have the variety of fish that Lake Tanganyika does.

The best place to stay is the Lake Mweru Water Transport Guest House in Nchelenge. It is a grey and white building down on the waterfront very close to the municipal rest house. It is very reasonable indeed with spotlessly clean, if somewhat bizarrely furnished, rooms with en-suite bathrooms. The complex is generally self-catering, but simple meals of *nshima* and fresh bream can be arranged.

The beach where the fishermen land their catches early each morning is a short walk from here and the ensuing gathering that comes to buy kapenta and bream is a colourful spectacle.

Lake Mweru Wantipa

Lake Mweru Wantipa lies directly between lakes Mweru and Tanganyika. Falling mostly within a national park, it has been covered on page 124. It is worth noting that some maps, such as the green Republic of Zambia Tourist Map, have overprinted the lake so that it appears to be some kind of marsh. It is in fact an open lake, although subject to unusual changes in level in drought cycles.

Lake Tanganyika

Lake Tanganyika is perhaps the best known of Zambia's lakes, being by far the largest and most interesting. Although Zambia can only lay claim to about 7 per cent of the lake, it revels in sharing its statistics. Lake Tanganyika is the longest and seventh largest lake in the world. It is the second biggest lake in Africa after Lake Victoria and the second deepest lake in the world after Lake Baikal in Russia. It has a surface area of 32 914 sq km and is 1 395 m deep, which is 642 m below sea level!

Lake Tanganyika is of course part of the Great Rift Valley, which explains its immense depth and the steep topography of its shoreline, which is so different from other lakes in the country. Consequently the Zambian shore is far less populated than Lake Mweru. In addition a considerable length of the shore falls within Sumbu National Park (see page 125) and so remains relatively wild and unspoiled. Only the top 200 m or so of the lake has oxygen. The relationship between those vast somnolent depths and the richly animated surface is still being studied, but it seems that chemical interaction between them is responsible for the incredible richness and variety of life forms in the lake. Scientists studying the lake say they have not even documented all the species of fish to be found there. The majority are small cichlids and the like. Some are brilliantly hued and are caught for the pet trade, but what makes anglers' eyes gleam is the number of sporting fish. These are the southernmost waters in which Goliath tigerfish and Nile perch are found.

There are three lodges on the Sumbu side of the lake. The two inside the national park have been described above. The only camping facility here is to be found at Ndole Bay Lodge, which is reached by turning left 5 km before the gate at Sumbu. The 8 km access road is frightful but the lodge itself is pleasant and beautifully situated above a small beach where the absence of crocodiles makes swimming and other water sports possible. The lodges hire boats and guides to prospective fishermen. For those with their own boats the only proper launching ramp is at Kasaba Bay, but getting the boat there on the road in its present state is likely to be something of an ordeal.

Note that there is no direct vehicular route between Sumbu and Mpulungu. By boat it is about 80 km. By car it is necessary to drive all the way back to Mporokoso and then proceed towards Kasama for another 81,6 km, where just as you pass a stand of tall eucalyptus trees a road veers off to the left. This is a shortcut obviating the need to go all the way to Kasama and it joins the Kasama-Mbala road after 71 km, 75 km from Mbala. Total distance is 320 km.

Before independence Mbala was called Abercorn. There are two hotels: the Grasshopper Inn and the Arms Hotel (formerly the Abercorn Arms). Nearby is Lake Chilwa, which is picturesque and said to be safe for swimming. While in Mbala it is very worthwhile visiting the Motomoto Museum which has interesting archaeological and indigenous cultural artifacts as well as colonial memorabilia.

A few kilometres south of Mbala there is a turning to Mpulungu some 40 km down the escarpment on the shore of Lake Tanganyika. Mpulungu is landlocked Zambia's "port". Here the big lake ferries from Bujumbura in Burundi and Kigoma in Tanzania dock. There is also a thriving fishing industry, but the town owes its existence to the passage of trucks on and off the ferries. There is only one place to stay – Nkupe Lodge. This is a self-catering facility really aimed at backpackers that is pleasantly low-key and inexpensive.

The only real reason for travellers to come to Mpulungu is to embark on one of the northbound ferries. Recently, however, a couple has opened a small camp a few kilometres west of Mpulungu offering snorkelling safaris. If you are spending a day in Mpulungu follow the track past Nkupe Lodge for about 150 m to the ruins of the Niamkolo Church. It is the oldest "surviving" stone church in Zambia. In 1880 (only seven years after Livingstone's death, when the territory had barely been explored by Europeans) the London Missionary Society established a mission at Niamkolo, while looking for a site on the southern end of the lake to assemble and launch a steamboat, the SS *Good News*. In the face of aggression from Arab slave traders they had to abandon the site. The British in Nyasaland to the south-east were meanwhile putting paid to the nefarious trade and in 1887 the missionaries returned to Niamkolo. In 1893 Alfred J Swann bought a piece of land and in 1895 work was started on the church. One Adam Purves, a helper at the mission, is said to have been the architect. The walls were built by building two skins of rough-hewn stone almost a yard apart and then filling the gap in between with rubble. Both nave and tower were roofed with thatch. The high incidence of sleeping sickness however led to the mission being moved in 1908, and shortly afterwards it burned to the ground. There is something poignant in the thought that after so much work the church was probably in use for barely two years. In 1962 the walls were rebuilt and the cement grouting dates from this time.

If you have a boat or can organise one you could go out to Kituta Bay, east of Mpulungu, where lies the hull of the other missionary enterprise, the *SS Good News*. The 54-foot ship was originally built in England and delivered to the mouth of the Zambezi from where it sailed up to the Shire River, where in places it had to be carried, then sailed the length of Lake Nyasa (Malawi) to Karonga where it was dismantled and then carried 400 km overland to Lake Tanganyika. Because Niamkolo was being threatened by Arabs the boat was carried to the Lufubu River, where after a year of reassembly it was launched in 1895. There is a monument on the site to commemorate the event. The *Good News* remained in service for many years. Her propeller and flag can be seen in the Moto-moto museum in Mbala.

By far the most impressive spectacle in the vicinity and definitely worth the excursion is the Kalambo Falls. Here the Kalambo River – which at this point marks the boundary between Zambia and Tanzania – plunges 221 m in the second highest single-drop waterfall on the continent. That is more than twice the height of the Victoria Falls. To see this when the river is in flood in February must be an awesome sight. In the dry season it is impressive enough. The gorge itself is almost 300 m deep and sheer-sided at the fall. These cliffs are a nesting site for marabou storks, who add a sense of primeviality to the spectacle as they soar like pterodactyls above the plunging waters. The falls are accessible by car. Take the road north out of Mbala and then turn left as signposted. The falls are 33 km from Mbala and the road is poor, becoming terrible towards the end. For this reason you may have to walk the last couple of hundred metres. If you do so, lock your car and preferably leave someone to watch it. Apparently there are bandits from

Tanzania who may otherwise help themselves to your belongings. Another way to see the falls that is more fun but requires a little fitness is to hire a boat at Mpulungu which will take you round to the river and a little way upstream. Then it is a walk of a few kilometres to the foot of the falls and a good hike up to the top. For backpackers the cheapest and perhaps most exciting way to see the falls is to take one of the water taxis that ply between Tanzania and Mpulungu. They will drop you at the river mouth on one day and collect you the next. Take basic camping gear and sleep next to the river.

OTHER PLACES TO SEE

There are several other waterfalls in the northern region of Zambia that are worth making the effort to see. Many make ideal places to camp en route and some even have camping sites nearby that are clean and little used.

The Kundalila Falls are easily accessible to most travellers driving up into northern Zambia, as they are just off the Great North Road at Kanona about 20 km north of the Mansa road junction. A signposted track goes east from the road for 13 km. Just before the falls picnic site there is a boom across the road where you need to sign in. The Kaombe River is a clear stream which gurgles out of a pretty meadow and then suddenly slides and shoots over a 65-m drop to fall into a clear pool that invites an invigorating swim. There is a path to the bottom of the fall. The view from the top out over the distant Luangwa Valley is one of the loveliest in Zambia. There are contradictory notices about whether camping is allowed here.

Military installations in the vicinity have made it a sensitive area and the former government disallowed camping. In the author's experience camping is now allowed but visitors are warned that the caretaker may use the ambiguous situation to extort money out of prospective campers. A small payment for upkeep of the site is advised, but no more.

The Chishimba Falls near Kasama are an ideal place to camp. About 18,5 km out on the road from Kasama to Luwingu there is a right turn to Mporokoso and about 5 km up that road, as it reaches the top of a small hill, a sign marking the Chishimba Falls power station points left down a small road leading directly into the campsite. The falls actually consist of three falls. Above two of them weirs have been placed to channel water to a hydro-electric plant. All this engineering has in fact been done quite discreetly and does not spoil the scenery much. First the Mutumuna Falls crash down onto pitch-black rocks before flowing into a small clear lake made by the weir above the Kevala Falls. The Kevala Falls tumble over a series of rocks and then slide magnificently over a huge slab of rock as the Chishimba Falls. Then the river tumbles through a pretty gorge covered in evergreen forest. The campsite has a roofed cooking area and a pit latrine.

The Chipoma Falls near Chinsali are really just a series of large rapids which may be worth stopping to see en route between Mpika and Tunduma. To get there turn west off the Great North Road about 57 km after the Shiwa Ngandu turnoff or 24 km south of the Chinsali turnoff. Drive about 6 km, keeping left at forks and junctions.

To get to the spectacular Kundabwika Falls you need to take the road from Mporokoso to Kawambwa, and 64 km out a road turns north to Mununga on Lake Mweru. Some 40 km up this road a left turn leads directly to the falls on the Kalungwishi River, which at this point marks the northern boundary of the Lusenga Plain National Park.

From here the Kalungwishi River flows down the eastern boundary of the national park until it plunges over the most magnificent falls in the region, the Lumangwe Falls. To see these take the road west from Mporokoso for 84 km toward Kawambwa where, just 2 km east of the Chimpembe Pontoon, a road turns to the right or northwest. There is a picket where you have to sign in and then it is 13 km to the falls. There is an abandoned rest house near the falls where visitors are welcome to camp. There is an even better spot to camp literally metres from the lip of the falls. It would be well worth spending a night here. Thirty metres high and easily 120 m across, these falls are in every way just a scaled-down version of the Victoria Falls and the surrounding forest is beautiful.

The Ntumbachushi Falls on the Ng'ona River are about 15 km west of Kawambwa towards Kazembe where the access road turns back south-east for about a kilometre. The falls are lovely and indeed the whole area is very scenic. For a small charge visitors can camp at the falls. There are latrines and the caretaker will provide firewood.

The Livingstone Memorial is really only worth a visit if you are in the immediate area, either at Kasanka or going into the Bangweulu. The memorial is rather uninspiring, but it is moving to stand at the spot where the great explorer finally met his end. David Livingstone started out on his last African journey in 1866. He travelled up Lake Malawi then explored westwards to lakes Tanganyika, Mweru and Bangweulu. For six years no news of him reached the outside world until the journalist turned explorer, Henry Morton Stanley, met him at the town of Ujiji on the eastern shores of Lake Tanganyika with the now famous words: "Dr Livingstone, I presume." Thereafter Livingstone headed west and south in search of the elusive source of the Nile. He could not have known that it lay in precisely the opposite direction.

At Lake Bangweulu Livingstone was delayed by floods and, unable to progress, fell steadily more ill with dysentery. Eventually he was carried through the swamps to the village of Chief Chitambo, where he died kneeling beside his bed. His bearers and servants then buried his entrails beneath a tree that stood just where the memorial stands today. His body was salted and dried in the sun for a fortnight before his servants, in the most extraordinary gesture of devotion, carried it 1 500 km to the coast at Bagamoyo. From there it was shipped back to England to be buried in Westminster Abbey.

Route 10: The Great North Road. Kapiri Mposhi via Mpika, Kasama to Mbala and Mpulungu

Distance: 812 km. Time: 15 hours.
Potholed tar.
Petrol not always reliable at Kapiri but usually available at Serenje, Mpika and Kasama.
Recommended stay-over: Kapishya Springs or Kasanka, Kundalila Falls, Chishimba Falls.

At Kapiri Mposhi the road and the railway line from Livingstone and Lusaka fork and the Great North Road proceeds towards east Africa. As one might expect from such a major junction, Kapiri is a rough truckers' town of dosshouses and nightspots. These vie for the attentions of the passing traffic with colourful murals. You might stop for a *mosi* and *nshima* with road-kill chicken, but it is unlikely you would care to spend the night. Just 5 km from town turn east past the Chimulangi Nightspot. It is then 192 km to Serenje, bypassing Mkushi and coming very close to the Zaïre border, after which the road begins a gentle ascent up onto the Zambezi-Zaïre watershed. This section of the road, particularly in the region of Mkushi, has become appallingly potholed in recent years. Major roadworks will become necessary in the near future. In the meantime drive cautiously. The trucks coming the other way veer round the potholes like great lurching juggernauts with scant regard for any smaller oncoming traffic.

There are two motels in Serenje, but both are noisy and a better option if you need somewhere to spend the night would be to camp at the Kundalila Falls, 60 km further on. Forty kilometres from Serenje is the turnoff to the left of the Chinese-built road to Mansa which is the way to Kasanka and Bangweulu. At Kanona the track that turns down to Kundalila Falls is signposted, but not clearly so ask locals if unsure. The falls are 13 km down the track. Note that under the previous regime camping was not allowed, but for a small fee the caretaker will let you do so. The other place worth stopping to have a look is the Nsalu Cave with its remarkable rock paintings. To reach it turn west off the Great North Road 30 km north of Kanona then proceed 7 km to where the caretaker, Mr Thomas Mambwe, lives. After a further 7 km a road turns south to the cave. The cave is fenced off but the paintings can be clearly seen. Visitors wishing to go right into the cave to examine the paintings must be accompanied by the caretaker.

Mpika is 236 km from Serenje. Just before Mpika the road forks. The Great North Road proceeds through Mpika to Isoka, 260 km away, and Tunduma on the Tanzanian border 109 km beyond that.

Note that you cannot count on buying petrol at Isoka and for those travelling through, petrol will probably only be available at Mbeya in Tanzania.

The turnoff to Shiwa Ngandu which proceeds through to Kapishya Hot Springs is 89 km up the Great North Road from the Mpika road junction. This road eventually joins the Mpika-Kasama road some 86 km north of Mpika. The road to Kasama crosses the Chambeshi River about 35 km beyond this point. At the north end of the old bridge there is a monument marking the spot where the hostilities of the First World War were brought to an end when the legendary commander of the German Forces in east Africa, General von Lettow Vorbeck, surrendered to Mr Hector Croad, British District Commissioner, at Mpika on 14 November 1918, three days after armistice of which the Germans were unaware. The artillery piece in the memorial is a breech-loading field gun of the kind used by German forces in that campaign. The war in east Africa that this concluded was perhaps the last "gentlemen's war" in history and well worth reading up on.

Ninety kilometres beyond the bridge lies the town of Kasama, administrative capital of the region. Kasama has banks, petrol and a hotel. Travellers wishing to camp near here should proceed to the Chishimba Falls.

From Kasama one can turn east to Isoka 175 km away, west to Lu-wingu 150 km away and Mporokoso 160 km away or proceed north on the main road to Mbala, which is 167 km from Kasama. Only the Mbala road is tarred.

Just a few kilometres before Mbala a left turn marks the 40 km road down the escarpment to Mpulungu.

11 THE EASTERN REGION

THE LUANGWA VALLEY

The eastern region of Zambia consists almost entirely of the Luangwa Valley drainage system between the Muchinga Escarpment and the hills of Malawi and Mozambique. And the primary reason for visitors to go there is to visit the magnificent Luangwa Valley and the game reserves that have made the valley such a famous wildlife sanctuary and tourist destination. It covers a large region of the country yet it is serviced by only one major road – The Great East Road (GER), which runs from Lusaka to Lilongwe in Malawi via Petauke and Chipata. Only minor roads connect towns further north, such as Lundazi, to the GER. The Great East Road is tarred and both Lilongwe and the main gate of the South Luangwa National Park are easily accessible in normal cars, but for any diversions from that route four-wheel-drive is recommended.

Game protection in the Luangwa Valley has a long history. In the late 19th century elephant and hippo were heavily exploited by the Chikunda tribe from Mozambique as well as Arabs based on Lake Malawi. Hippo were at one stage so rare that the British South Africa Company which administered the territory imposed a total ban on hunting them until their numbers recovered. Nowadays the area positively teems with hippo.

With the establishment of the British South Africa Company administration in 1898 and control over elephant hunting, elephant numbers started to recover. The BSAC established the first game reserve in the valley in the Luamfwa region in 1904 to protect the last remaining population of Thornicroft's giraffe. Although this reserve was subsequently deproclaimed in 1911, elephant populations continued to recover, and did so well that by 1930 they were becoming a serious problem for local subsistence farmers. Contracts were issued to men who were to become legendary "white hunters", such as Charlie Ross, Bill Langham and Freddy Hall, to shoot marauding elephants. Hall was mauled by a lion while trying to capture giraffe and died of his injuries.

Charlie Ross was killed by an elephant in 1938. In 1939 Ross was replaced by a young man, Norman Carr, who perhaps more than any other figure can be said to be the father of conservation in Zambia and particularly of the Luangwa Valley. (And he is still actively campaigning for the wildlife cause and passing on the wisdom accumulated over half a century from his home and lodge, Kapani.) At the same time the three major game reserves, North and South Luangwa and Lukusuzi were proclaimed.

In 1950 Norman Carr proposed a scheme whereby the local population could become involved in conservation and benefit from it. He persuaded Chief Nsefu to turn some of his tribal land into a private game reserve. Revenue from the reserve was returned to the chief's administration. The project was so successful that the Chewa asked that a camp be established at Luambe, which was done in 1954. In the late 1950s tourist camps were established and after retiring from government service in 1961 Carr and a partner, Peter Hankin, established the first safari company in the country. The tourist infrastructure was extended by the building of all-weather roads in the 1970s. Bridges over the Luangwa were constructed, as was the present airstrip. In 1972 all game reserves were abolished and designated national parks. A census in the early 1970s revealed an elephant population of over 100 000, but from about 1975 onwards poaching began to escalate dramatically. In 1980 the Save the Rhino Trust was established to combat poaching. In 1987 the Luangwa Independent Rural Development Project (LIRDP) was established, to implement an overall management policy for the Luangwa Valley and direct revenues accrued through tourism to the benefit of the local population.

SOUTH LUANGWA NATIONAL PARK

The most famous game reserve in the country, this is a magnificent park with abundant wildlife and a range of lodges and safari operations to cater for most budgets and travel tastes.

Location: The Luangwa River runs right through the eastern part of Zambia and almost the whole valley is given over to wildlife management. South Luangwa National Park covers 9 050 square kilometres between the west bank of the river and the Muchinga Escarpment. Safaris and lodges are concentrated on the river, the majority based on the east bank and conducting daily walks and drives across the river in the park.

How to get there: Safari operators can meet clients in Lusaka. There is an airstrip just outside Mfuwe, the main gate, and national and charter airlines make regular flights. A weekly flight from Lilongwe in Malawi is being considered.

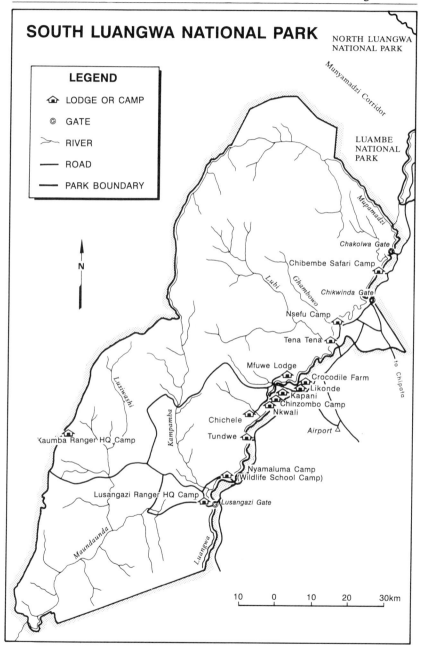

SOUTH LUANGWA NATIONAL PARK

NORTH LUANGWA NATIONAL PARK

LEGEND

⌂ LODGE OR CAMP

◎ GATE

⌇ RIVER

— ROAD

— PARK BOUNDARY

Munyamadzi Corridor

LUAMBE NATIONAL PARK

Mupamadzi

Chakolwa Gate

Chibembe Safari Camp

Chikwinda Gate

Nsefu Camp

Tena Tena

Mfuwe Lodge

Crocodile Farm

Likonde

Kapani

Chinzombo Camp

Nkwali

Chichele

Tundwe

Airport

Kaumba Ranger HQ Camp

Nyamaluma Camp
(Wildlife School Camp)

Lusangazi Ranger HQ Camp

Lusangazi Gate

N

Lubi

Ghambowo

Lusiwashi

Kampamba

Maundaunda

Luangwa

to Chipata

10   0   10   20   30km

By road Mfuwe is about 698 km from Lusaka. Follow the Great East Road to Petauke, from which four-wheel-drivers can follow a slow but scenically beautiful road straight to the park. Those without four-wheel-drive vehicles should proceed to Chipata and turn left just before the independence archway. (See Route 11 at the end of this chapter.) The park itself has some all-weather roads and is suitable for normal cars although, particularly in the wet season, a four-wheel-drive may be more comfortable.

Hitchhikers will find the going slow but there is enough traffic to and from Chipata to get you through. At the moment it is really the only national park accessible to hitchhikers at all.

What to see: The Luangwa Valley is part of the famous Rift Valley. To most visitors the Muchinga Escarpment will remain just a blue haze in the west. But between the Luangwa River and the escarpment lies a vast savanna sanctuary. Despite the endemic poaching of the 1980s there remains a fantastic amount of game. All the "big five" are readily seen except rhino. There is considerable doubt whether any rhino at all remain alive in Zambia and if they do their whereabouts is either unknown or kept highly secret. Predators are common and South Luangwa is particularly known for leopard sightings. The elephant population is but a fragment of the 100 000-strong population of the 1970s, but small family groups are frequently seen and if the devastation still visible in some areas is anything to go by, the drastic reduction in population may have a beneficial affect on the environment in the long term.

Antelope include impala, puku, eland, Lichtenstein's hartebeest, kudu and common waterbuck. It is interesting that this, the species of waterbuck found elsewhere in southern Africa, is quite different from the Defassa waterbuck found in the Kafue region. Of particular note is that the park is one of only two in the country where giraffe occur naturally, and those found here are a unique subspecies, the Thornicroft's giraffe, which has different markings from giraffe elsewhere. Cookson's wildebeest is also a subspecies of blue wildebeest and unique to the valley.

Botanical variation between broad-leafed woodland, acacia, mopane, grassy plains and huge riverine trees along the sandy river make the valley a paradise for birds, and almost 400 species have been recorded. Specialities are the Pel's fishing owl, large numbers of African skimmers, the African broadbill and as many as 40 different birds of prey.

When to go: Open all year, although many of the private lodges are closed during the rainy season. Best between April and October, although October can be suicidally hot.

Where to stay: There are two lodges inside the park, Mfuwe and Chichele, which were nationalised years ago and run by the NHDC. Now that that organisation has ceased to exist management has shifted to the wildlife service. They are less exclusive than the private lodges across the river and old-fashioned, but open all year. Management is likely to be privatised in the near future. For now they are best suited to the middle-budget, unfussy traveller who wishes to remain independent. Note that some lodges listed in tourist leaflets and maps are no longer operational or are being renovated.

Then there are a number of excellent upmarket lodges sporadically located along the east bank of the Luangwa River where they overlook the Park. Most of these are best booked in advance. Many of these lodges are owned and run by experts on conservation in Zambia, whose vast experience of the bush makes their guidance into the ways of the wild an experience worth every penny. Game drives are conducted in the park by experienced and knowledgeable guides and walks are additionally accompanied by armed scouts. Also, several lodges run bush camps in more remote corners of the park from which walking safaris are conducted. Walking safaris from bush camps are restricted to the dry season and some lodges close for the rains. The map shows the positions of the various lodges.

Not far south of Mfuwe is Kapani, run by Norman Carr Safaris and open all year. Kapani has a luxurious, old-fashioned atmosphere and there is a swimming pool. In the dry season Kapani runs two bush camps inside the Park – Luwi and Nsolo, where the emphasis is on game walks although some drives are undertaken.

Chinzombo, close to Kapani, is owned by the Save the Rhino Trust and is a medium-sized thatched lodge in a very scenic location. Chinzombo runs two bush camps, Chamilandu and Kuyenda, which sleep only six people in rustic but comfortable huts. The bush camps are dry-season-only but Chinzombo is only closed between January and April.

Robin Pope Safaris have two small and exclusive main camps on the east side of the river. Tena Tena is a tented camp and actually inside the Park where it encloses what was once called the Nsefu Game Reserve. Six large tents each have en-suite flush toilets and showers. It is open in the dry season only. Nkwali is south of Kapani and Chinzombo on private land overlooking the Luangwa River. This is a beautiful camp with six chalets which superbly combine modern comforts with a sense of being open to the wilds. Nkwali has a longer season, only closing for the very wet months of December through March.

Robin Pope Safaris also run walking safaris over five days in the remote and inaccessible Munyamadzi River region of the Park.

John Coppinger's Wilderness Safaris have two camps on the east bank of the Luangwa. Chibembe is 54 km north of the Mfuwe road. It has 40 beds in single, double and family sized wooden chalets with en-suite facilities. The camp is located over a large hippo pool in the river and there is always game to see from the terrace and a swimming pool to wallow in during the heat of the day. Nsefu Camp, the oldest tourist camp in Zambia, is inside the park boundaries. It has six twin-bedded thatched rondavels with en-suite facilities, close to a waterhole, so there is plenty of game in and around the camp. Wilderness Safaris also run five bush camps, three in the park, one on the Mupamadzi and one in the North Luangwa National Park.

Derek Shenton runs Kaingo Camp, which is a bush camp.

Sobek run a slightly less sophisticated camp, Tundwe Camp, some 25 km south of the Mfuwe road and so quite isolated. Six reed-matted chalets share two flush toilets and two hot-water showers. Sobek also run two bush camps that are available for walking safaris.

Camping is available close to the main gate outside the park at privately run campsites such as the Croc Farm and Flat Dogs campsite next to the crocodile farm, which also has a few chalets. For those not in their own vehicles, or if desired, game drives can be arranged. James Schultz's Likonde Camp has camping and self-catering chalets, but has been closed for renovation. The list above is not exhaustive. There are other safari companies building new camps or renovating old ones at a brisk rate, so you are well advised to contact travel agents and the Tour Operators Association for up-to-date information. For further details, booking, etc., see chapters 12 and 13.

NORTH LUANGWA NATIONAL PARK

This truly magnificent wilderness, surely one of the wildest places left on earth, is something of a special case and entry is restricted to two or three safari companies.

Location: The park lies north of "South Park" (obviously), the major game areas being on the Luangwa and its tributary the Mwaleshi River.

How to get there: Visitors may only go into the "North Park" under the auspices of one of the safari companies operating there. Shiwa Safaris (see Shiwa Ngandu, chapter 10) are the longest-standing operators in the park. They bring visitors from the stately manor house at Shiwa Ngandu near Mpika down the Muchinga Escarpment, either on foot or in four-wheel-drive vehicles, to their two simple bush camps on the Mwaleshi River. John Coppinger's Wilderness Safaris have a bush camp further downstream and access the park from the South Luangwa, where they run Chibembe Camp. Chris Wienand of Mwaleshi Safaris has also secured rights to operate in the park. These trips are four-wheel-drive journeys that take several hours. However Shiwa Ngandu is accessible by normal vehicle and Wilderness Safaris will arrange transfers from Mfuwe to Chibembe for guests unwilling to risk ordinary cars on the rough road to Chibembe. Transfers by plane or vehicle to both from Lusaka can be arranged.

What to see: Similar in terms of game and vegetation to the South Luangwa, this park's particular attraction is its remoteness. For the price of limiting access to the companies mentioned above, the park offers an unrivalled exclusivity. Once encamped beneath mahogany and Kigelia trees above the glimmering shallow water of the Mwaleshi River, you have 4 636 square kilometres all to yourselves, a superabundance of game and stars. There are lions aplenty and some of the biggest herds of buffalo in Africa. The authors have seen herds of up to 2 000 buffalo here.

There is excellent birdlife as well. Safaris are usually exclusive to one's own party. It is categorically one of the best safari destinations on the continent. The North Luangwa has been brought to the world's attention by Mark and Delia Owens, whose book *The Eye of the Elephant* (or *Survivor's Song* in South Africa) chronicles their struggle to preserve the park from poaching.

When to go: Safaris only operate during the dry season, late May to mid-October. The later in the season the better the game viewing. October is very hot.

Where to stay: There are no facilities other than those belonging to the above safari companies. These camps are in keeping with traditional bush camps elsewhere. Rebuilt every dry season, they consist of thatch walled and roofed bungalows on earth floors. There are proper beds and linen. Ablution facilities are usually en-suite but basic with a pit latrine and bucket showers.

The Owens are thinking of developing the park, which may see the leasing of rights to further camps along the east bank of the Luangwa

River. In the interests of preserving the park's very special quality of remoteness it is to be hoped that any such plans will be carried out with the utmost circumspection.

LUAMBE NATIONAL PARK

Location: Just north of the South Luangwa and on the east side of the river.

How to get there: Proceed north about 80 km from Mfuwe, past the turnoffs to Tena Tena and Chibembe camps. A scout camp and boom across the road mark the beginning of the park.

What to see: This is a very beautiful park, similar to the South Luangwa but with more spectacular trees, if somewhat less game because of hunting around the park. However it has a greater feeling of remoteness because there are no safari operations in the park. The old lodge is derelict. The only road is appalling; unbelievably bumpy in the dry season, the black cotton soil becomes a sticky quagmire in the wet. Although maps make the road look prominent, it is in fact just a track and travellers over it may easily think they are lost. Four-wheel-drive is essential.

When to go: May to October. It is likely that the roads will be impassable at any other time.

Where to stay: No facilities at present. Check with the NPWS when and whether camping might be allowed.

LUKUSUZI NATIONAL PARK

This park is also in the Luangwa Valley but some distance east of the Luangwa River. At the time of writing it has no facilities whatever and because of poaching the state of the game population is uncertain.

There are plans for development, however, and curious visitors should direct enquiries about possible safaris to the Tour Operators Association of Zambia, Box 30263, Lusaka, or for private visits, the National Parks and Wildlife Service.

Location: Between the Luangwa River and the Chipata-Lundazi road.

How to get there: Take the Great East Road then proceed past Chipata toward Lundazi for about 110 km. Turn left down a poor dirt road which traverses the park. The condition of the road in the park is uncertain. It is probably suitable for four-wheel-drive vehicles only. **What to see:** The game status here is uncertain. Big game may be encountered but is likely to be extremely wary because of poaching. **When to go:** The park is open all year but summer visitors should drive with caution. **Where to stay:** There are no facilities at present. Ask the game scouts at the gates for advice.

THE NYIKA PLATEAU and NATIONAL PARK

This is also something of a special case because it can only be reached via Malawi.

Location: The Nyika Plateau straddles the border between Malawi and Zambia right in the north-east of the country.

How to get there: The only road up onto the Nyika Plateau is in Malawi, so you have to cross over to that country in order to reach the park. There are three possible crossings. You can go directly from Chipata via Lilongwe and Kasungu. Although this is the longest way round on the map, it definitely has the best roads.

Alternatively from Chipata drive up through Lundazi before crossing the border and proceeding through Mzuzu and then Rumphi. The main road west from Rumphi goes directly to the park gate.

The third alternative, which is the most direct but probably takes the longest, is to remain in Zambia after Lundazi, driving all the way up through some quite remote country to the border gate at Katumbi, which is west of Rumphi and very close to the Nyika access road. Note that the Zambian border post at Katumbi can also be reached from Kasama via Isoka. If coming up from Lundazi it is easy to miss the Zambian post because the last junction is on the Malawian side of the boom. Turn left for 100 m at that junction. From the Zambian post it is then 8 rough kilometres to the Malawian post.

Both these last-mentioned routes are on poor roads that take a long time to travel and will probably necessitate camping along the way. Remember that you will have to undergo all the usual border formalities, whichever route you take. It is a long way to the Nyika from anywhere in Zambia and you will have to plan time carefully, bearing poor roads in mind if you are to make the National Park gates in Malawi before they close at 6 pm. Also you will need some local currency to pay the gate fees of 7,5 Malawi kwacha per vehicle and K3 per person per day. There is a bank in Rumphi where you can change dollars, pound or rands into Malawi kwacha. They will not accept Zambian kwacha.

What to see: The Nyika Plateau is quite unlike anywhere else in central Africa. Once one has climbed up the mountain pass, gone through the gate and passed through the broad-leafed woodland of the lower slopes, the plateau opens up into great rolling moors interspersed with patches of thick and deep montane forest. There is no actual border control between Zambia and Malawi once on the plateau, and in fact all internal routes and game drives are in Malawi. Game also tends to stick to Malawi territory, being safe there from Zambian poachers. And the game is fantastic. Antelope species such as roan, eland and reedbuck are found in large numbers. It is a particularly unusual environment in which to see roan and one is able to do so at close quarters. Other animals visitors are likely to see include blue monkey, bushbuck, blue duiker, red duiker and leopard. Nyika is said to have the highest concentration of leopard per square kilometre in Africa and visitors have a better than even chance of seeing one. Right on the northern side of the plateau lion, elephant and buffalo are apparently also found. The best way to see them is to hire a guide and bearers at Chilanda Camp and do a walking safari over several days to that northern area.

When to go: Open all year. Best game viewing is said to between November and May although February and March are very wet and a four-wheel-drive vehicle is recommended.

Where to stay: The reason Nyika is included in this guide at all is that the Zambian Rest House is situated on the Zambian edge of the plateau. With all the unsophisticated grace of a bygone era this is a perfect place to spend a few days far – very far – from the madding crowd. It is now run by Robin Pope Safaris, who use it for their own Nyika expeditions, but when not in use it can be booked by other self-catering travellers. You will be expected to hand over your supplies to Mr Gondwe, the manager-cum-chef, who will then cook for you and serve your meals on Federation silver. Starched napkins, spotless sheets on the beds and boiling hot water in the bathrooms all make the Zambian Rest House unforgettable. But if you need cheaper accommodation or camping facilities the main Malawian camp, Chilanda, is not far away.

Walking from the rest house is permissible and one can spend hours hiking in these game-rich dales or trout fishing in the clear streams that run through them.

Route 11: Lusaka to South Luangwa National Park via Great East Road to Chipata

Distance: 569 km to Chipata then 120 to the main gate.
Petrol: Nyimba, Petauke, Katete, Chipata.

The Great East Road begins at Cairo Road's north end circle and departs Lusaka via the agricultural showgrounds, the University of Zambia and the airport. Between the university and the airport lies the last petrol station, beyond which the next available fuel is likely to be at Nyimba or Petauke, 328 km and 394 km from Lusaka respectively. So fill tanks accordingly. This is one of the better roads in the country, tar all the way to Chipata with relatively few potholes. About 100 km out of town the road enters into pretty, undulating country. It is 162 km to Rufunsa. Then the road begins to descend to the Luangwa River. Beautiful as the bridge and valley is, be careful when taking photographs; there is usually a military roadblock in the vicinity. From Rufunsa it is 65 km to the bridge and then 60 km to Kachalola where petrol may be available. Then it is 42 km to Nyimba and 68 km from there to Petauke. About 12 km before Katete a turnoff left to the Zambia National Service Farm takes one a few kilometres to the national monument site, the Mkoma Rock shelter, where there is a series of stylistic rock paintings dating from the Iron Age. From Katete it is 88 km to Chipata, but travellers proceeding to the South Luangwa should turn left immediately before the independence memorial archway on the outskirts of the town.

From here on the road is a dirt road likely to be very corrugated if it has not been graded recently. It is 67 km to the Chisengu turnoff. Proceed left. The right-hand road, which appears on the map to be a shortcut to Chibembe Lodge, is in very bad condition and not recommended. Thereafter it is 15,7 km to Jumbe, where the road again forks to the left over a bridge. It is almost 17 km to the Mfuwe airport turnoff. Proceed straight on for nearly 6 km to the Catholic church. Here the road forks again. Travellers proceeding to the main gate at Mfuwe and the lodges south of it should keep left then turn right at the T-junction. Travellers proceeding northwards to Tena Tena, Nsefu or Chibembe can take a small shortcut by turning right opposite the church and proceeding over a bridge. Those going north should be aware that four-wheel-drive may be necessary from here on as several sandy riverbeds need to be crossed. Those proceeding the other way now get back onto tar and the road goes directly to the bridge and gate beyond which it is just a kilometre or so to Mfuwe. Just before the bridge a main road south goes down to Chinzombo, Kapani and Nkwali and opposite there is a signposted turn to the Croc Farm and Flatdogs campsite.

12 WHERE TO STAY

Accommodation in Zambia covers the full budget spectrum from the most luxurious to the positively penal. Top hotels have high standards, there are game lodges that are quite superb; middle-range hotels can be pricey for what they offer, but lodgings of one sort or another can be found in almost every town in the country, although their standards vary wildly. A feature of Zambia is that every town has a rest house run by the district or town council. While some of these have degenerated into brothels or shebeens, they are very cheap and some are quite acceptable with clean sheets and facilities. Travellers on tight budgets would do well to check them out.

Although the following list is as comprehensive as possible, it is restricted to places where tourists might possibly stop and generally excludes the ubiquitous government rest houses and bottom of the market, ungraded establishments. It bears repeating that the tourist industry in Zambia is burgeoning so rapidly that this book cannot hope to be absolutely up to date with developments and travellers should still consult travel agencies. Hotels in Zambia are given a "star" grading and lodges are graded alphabetically, "A" being top rated, "B", "C", etc., progressively lower graded. However visitors should not take these ratings entirely seriously, especially where lodges are concerned; having international colour televison in every bungalow is considered more important by Zambians than by visitors dying to get away from it all. So where necessary the official rating below is supplemented with a slightly more subjective assessment. Where such differences exist a division is made between upmarket, medium and low budget options.

Zambia's international dialling code is 260.

ACCOMMODATION IN AND AROUND TOWNS AND CITIES
Lusaka Area Code: 1

Upmarket
Holiday Inn Garden Court – Lusaka Ridgeway*
| Independence Ave | Box 30666 | Tel: 25-1666 | r155 |
| | Lusaka | Fax: 25-3529 | b215 |

Centrally located, recently taken over by the Holiday Inn group and revamped with conference facilities, casino, swimming pool.

Hotel Intercontinental****

Location	Address	Tel/Fax/Tlx	Rooms
Haile Selassie	Box 32201	Tel: 22-7911	r400
Avenue	Lusaka	Fax: 25-1880	b478
		Tlx: ZA251880	
		ZA41440	

An international-style hotel with most facilities including squash courts, swimming pool and casino.

Lilayi Lodge "B"

Lilayi,	Box 30098	Tel: 22-8682	r24
Kafue Rd	Lusaka	Fax: 22-2906	b36
		Tlx: ZA40536	

A pleasant out of town alternative, set on a game farm, but close enough to Lusaka for those with business there. Transfers arranged.

Pamodzi Hotel*****

Addis Ababa Dr	Box 35450	Tel: 22-7957/81	r202
	Lusaka	Fax: 25-0995	b408
		Tlx: ZA44720	

Lusaka's smartest hotel, 2 km from city centre. Banquet rooms, conference facilities, casino, forex, barber and beauty salons, pool, 2 squash courts, 2 tennis courts, a health club, etc.

Medium

Andrews Motel**

Kafue Rd,	Box 30475	Tel: 27-2532	r97
	Lusaka	Fax: 27-4798	b200

Rather noisy venue for local socialising, with swimming pool and tennis court.

Chainama Hotel***

Great East Rd	Box 51033	Tel: 29-2451/7	r28
	Lusaka	Fax: 29-0809	b56

Modern, halfway between city and airport. Pool, function rooms and facilities, rooms have private balconies.

Garden House Motel***

Mumbwa Rd	Box 30815	Tel: 28-9328	r50
	Lusaka	Fax: 28-7337	b100

Reasonably priced, convenient for those intending to visit the Kafue National Park, being 5 km from the city on the Mumbwa Rd.

The Hillview Hotel (ungraded)
Kafue Rd   Box 30815   Tel: 27-8554   r8
                  Lusaka   Fax: 22-9074   b12
Although new and so not yet graded, a clean, small hotel 20 minutes
from the city. Take the Kafue Rd and 1 km after Andrews Motel take
first tar road right and follow it for about 5 km.

Lusaka Hotel**
Cairo Rd   Box 30044   Tel: 22-9049   r79
                  Lusaka   Fax: 22-5726   b139
The only hotel conveniently in the centre of town, it is popular and
reasonably priced, but a little claustrophobic, noisy and chaotic.

Ndeke Hotel**
Cnr Haile Selassie   Box 30815   Tel: 25-2779   r44
& Saddam Hussein   Lusaka   Fax: 25-2779   b88
This reasonably priced hotel has a rather charming and vaguely ec-
centric atmosphere appropriate to a central African capital.

Fringilla Farm
Great North Rd   Box 31440   Tel (01) 611228   r7
Chisambu   Lusaka   b20
About an hour north of Lusaka. Tasteful bungalows, good food, and
a bustling farm atmosphere, ideal if heading north or on farming busi-
ness. Clean campsite with bungalows and hot water.

Budget

Fairview Hotel (ungraded)
Church Rd   Box 33200   Tel: 21-2954   r30
                  Lusaka   Tlx: ZA40572   b64
All rooms have colour TV – a feature considered by many Zambians
to be more important than a new coat of paint.

The Barn Motel*
Great East Rd   Box CH242   Tel: 282890/2   r50
                  Lusaka   Fax: 228949   b92
                                    Tlx: ZA48670
20 km from the city centre and 10 km from the airport.

Pre Cem Motel (ungraded)
Great North Rd   Box 30659   Tel: 21-3613/   r38
                  Lusaka   21-3314   b48
The nightclub and cocktail bar will – or perhaps won't – be an attraction.

Livingstone Area Code: 03

Upmarket

Mosi-Oa-Tunya Hotel (Intercontinental)*****
Victoria Falls Rd   Box 50151   Tel: 32-1121/9   r100
                      Livingstone   Tlx: ZA24221   b200
Splendidly, yet discreetly located virtually at the lip of the falls, 5-star amenities including squash courts, swimming pool and casino have not impinged on one of the greatest natural wonders of the world. Sleep with the sound of thunder in your ears.

Tongabezi Lodge "D"
17 km upriver   Pvt Bag 31   Tel: 32-3235   r7
Take Sesheke Rd   Livingstone   Fax: 32-3224
                                         Tlx: ZA24011   b14
An exquisite blend of sophistication and rusticity right on the banks of the Zambezi. All transfers to and from Livingstone are arranged as well as tours by plane or boat to the falls and tailored safaris. A feature is a picnic on Livingstone Island, literally at the Falls' edge.

Medium

New Fairmount Hotel**
Mosi-oa-Tunya Rd   Box 60096   Tel: 32-0726   r79
                      Livingstone   Tlx: ZA44720   b162
Right in the centre of Livingstone, 10 km from the only reason for being there, the Victoria Falls.

Rainbow Lodge "E"
Victoria Falls Rd   Box 60090   Tel: 32-1806   r26
                      Livingstone   b54
Superb location on the river. Main building tacky and run down, but new self-contained chalets.

Chundukwa Tree Lodge (ungraded)
30 km upriver   Tel: 32-3235   r3
on Sesheke Rd   Fax: 32-3224   b6
                                         Tlx: ZA24043
As yet ungraded, this pleasant camp has chalets built on stilts above the water; used as a base for Chundukwa Adventure Trails. Pick-ups from town, visits to the falls, canoe and other safaris arranged.

Wasawange Lodge & Tours
                      Box 60278   Tel: 32-4066
                      Livingstone   Fax: 32-4067
New and close to town.

Kubu Cabins (ungraded)
35 km upriver   Box 60748   Tel/Fax 324091
                       Livingstone
A new lodge with timber and thatch "cabins" offering an extensive package of activities on the river and around the falls. Also camping facilities.

Budget

Chalets Motel***
                  Box 60700   Tel: 2556/   r63
                  Livingstone   3570   b114
Located 1 km from airport.
Windsor Hotel (ungraded)
                  Box 60316   Tel: 32-1659   r35
                  Livingstone   b52
Busiku Farms (ungraded)
Signposted from Kateta Avenue.
A very basic campsite located on a farm about 11 km out of town. Part of the farm is being stocked with game.

Ndola Area code: 02

Upmarket

New Savoy Hotel****
Buteko Ave   Box 71800   Tel: 61-1097/8   r154
                  Ndola   Fax: 61-4001   b210
                                     Tlx: ZA30020
Centrally located, the smartest hotel on the Copperbelt boasts the only first-floor swimming pool in the country and a casino.

Medium

Mukuba Hotel***
Showgrounds   Box 72120   Tel: 65-5545/9   r50
                  Ndola   Fax: 65-5729   b90
                                     Tlx: ZA30077
Although tricky to find, (follow the signs into the agricultural showgrounds) this hotel has a very pleasant atmosphere with a few impala wandering around, well kept gardens and a very good restaurant.

Budget

New Ambassador Hotel (ungraded)

| President Ave | Box 71538 | Tel: 3038/ | r30 |
| | Ndola | 3103 | b54 |

Basic, but centrally located not far from the bus terminus.

Kitwe Area code: 02

Upmarket – none

Medium

Edinburgh Hotel**

| Cnr Independence | Box 21800 | Tel: 21-2188 | r78 |
| & Obote Ave | Kitwe | Fax: 22-5036 | b146 |

Somewhat run down from former splendour, but there's air-conditioning, a casino and swimming pool.

Nkana Hotel**

| Independence | Box 20664 | Tel: 22-4166 | r63 |
| Ave | Kitwe | | b110 |

Nice looking, set around a pleasant courtyard but slightly run down and apt to be very noisy, especially on weekends.

Budget

Buchi Hotel (ungraded)

| | Box 22495 | | r17 |
| | Kitwe | | b34 |

Chingola Area code: 02

Nchanga Motel*

| | Box 10024 | Tel: 31-2148 | r30 |
| | Chingola | | b54 |

The best of a poor choice. Well-known haunt for certain businesswomen.

Lima Motel (ungraded and insalubrious)

| Kitwe Rd | Box 10497 | Tel: 31-1894 | r27 |
| | Chingola | | b59 |

Musunsya Hotel (ungraded)

| | Box 10021 | Tel: 31-1115 | r30 |
| | Chingola | | b36 |

Mufulira Area code: 02

Mufulira Hotel**

Box 40727	Tel: 41-1477	r24
Mufulira		b48

Kamuchanga Hotel (ungraded)

Box 798	Tel: 41-2377	r25
Mufulira		b48

Masiye Motel (ungraded)

Box 40391		r84
Mufulira		b112

Mongu Area code: 07

Lyambai Hotel (ungraded)

Box 910198	Tel: 22-1271	r17
Mongu		b34

Outwardly uninspiring, but the hotel is clean and pleasant.

Ngulu Hotel*

Box 142	Tel: 22-1028	r16
Mongu		b28

Sir Mwanawina III Motel (ungraded)

	Tel: 22-1485	r54
		b81

Run by the district council and located on the Senanga road.

Senanga Area code: 07

Senanga Lodge (ungraded)

Box 920077		r16
Senanga		b36

As yet ungraded, pleasantly sited above the Zambezi.
Comfortable bungalows. Decent food. Rather noisy bar terrace.

Solwezi Area code: 08

Changa Changa Motel*

Chingola Rd	Box 110248	Tel: 82-1572	r28
	Solwezi		b48

Zambezi Area code: 08

Zambezi Motel (ungraded)

	Box 150001		r28
	Zambezi		b48

The magnificent view is unlikely to make up for less than salubrious facilities.

Mazabuka Area code: 032

Mazabuka Hotel (ungraded)

Main Rd	Box 670022	Tel: 3-0284	r16
	Mazabuka		b32

Choma Area code: 032

Choma Hotel (ungraded)

Main Rd	Box 63050	Tel: 2-0189	r20
	Choma		b38

Kalundu Hotel (ungraded)

	Box 630088		r40
	Choma		b76

Kabwe Area code: 05

Upmarket – none

Medium

Elephant's Head Hotel***

	Box 80410	Tel: 22-2522	r35
	Kabwe		b70

Masiye Motel**

	Box 81210	Tel: 22-3221	r66
	Kabwe		b112

Budget

Mulungushi Motel*

	Box 80408	Tel: 22-4602	r28
	Kabwe		b52

Swimming pool.

Horison Hotel (ungraded)
Box 80458   Tel: 22-3398   r18
Kabwe   b31

Kapiri Mposhi Area code: 05

Kapiri Motel (ungraded)
GNR   Box 13   Tel: 27-1148   r8
Kapiri Mposhi   b14
Unity Hotel (ungraded)
Box 59   Tel: 27-1350   r36
Kapiri Mposhi   b52
Rooms do have separate bathrooms.

Mansa Area code: 02

Mansa Hotel**
Box 710008   Tel: 82-1606   r30
Mansa   b60
Recently renovated.

Kasama Area code: 04

Upmarket – none

Medium

Modern Kwacha Relax Hotel**
Box 53   Tel: 22-1124   r32
Kasama   b56

Budget

Kasama Hotel (ungraded)
Box 165   Tel: 22-1188   r16
Kasama   b30

Mbala Area code: 04

Grasshopper Inn*
Box 93   Tel: 291   r14
Mbala   b26

Arms Hotel (ungraded)
Box Mbala r10
b20

Mpulungu Area code: 04

Nkupe Lodge (ungraded)
P/Bag 8 r4
Mpulungu b7
Aimed primarily at backpackers this pleasant, downmarket lodge offers
chalets and camping to self-catering travellers at very reasonable rates.

Chipata Area code: 062

Chipata District Council Motel*
Box 20 Tel: 21288 r30
Chipata b60
Crystal Springs Hotel (ungraded)
Box 510100 Tel: 21154 r40
Chipata b88

Lundazi Area code: 064

Lundazi Castle Motel (ungraded)
Box 530100 Tel: 8-0173 r12
Lundazi b24
Worth seeing for its sheer eccentricity, a colonial administrator's idea
of a Norman castle made to look all the more ridiculous by the trappings
of a low budget hotel.

Chirundu Area code: 01

Gwabi Lodge "C"
Box 30813 Tel: 25-0772 r6
b12
11 km east of Chirundu, turn right just after the border post; this simple
lodge set in lovely gardens on the Kafue River offering cheap camping
with decent ablution facilities or mid-priced chalets all inclusive, is
certainly the best bet for early and late border crossers. Used by Drifters
Canoe Safaris. Will help with minor vehicle repairs.

Nyambadwe Motel (ungraded)
           Box 33573   r12
           Lusaka   b12

Siavonga Area code: 01

Upmarket – none

Medium

Manchinchi Bay Lodge "A"
           Box 115   Tel: 51-1399   r30
           Siavonga   Tlx: ZA70903   b60
Well-kept gardens at the water's edge. Air-conditioned rooms with en-suite shower/toilet. Exclusive (and expensive) bar.

Zambezi Lodge (ungraded)
           Box 30   Tel: 5-1200   r25
           Siavonga   b50
Average facilities at upmarket prices.

Lake Kariba Inn (ungraded)
           Box 117   Tel: 51-1358/   r35
           Siavonga   51-1269   b70
Mainly caters for Lusaka's conference trade. An uninspiring appearance belies decent accommodation and dining facilities.

Sandy Beach
           Box 103   Tel: 01-511353
           Siavonga
Small, tented, personalised lodge 15 km west of Siavonga.

Budget

Eagles Rest Chalets "E"
           Box 1   Tel: 51-1168   r12
           Siavonga (Lusaka)   b50
Basic but comfortable in a pleasant setting.

Leisure Bay Motel (ungraded)
           Box 4   r14
           Siavonga   b28
Undergoing renovation

GAME LODGES IN AND AROUND NATIONAL PARKS

"NP" signifies that the lodge is located within the boundaries of the national park; "GMA" that the lodge lies in a Game Management Area just outside the national park. The former usually require park entry fees before proceeding to the lodge. In the latter these fees are arranged later or are included in the tariff. It is worth noting that previously state-owned lodges are being privatised, so ownership is likely to change and comments made here will become outdated.

Kafue National Park

Chunga Camp

GMA	Njovu Safaris	Being rebuilt
	Box 34250	
	Lusaka	

Chunga Safari Village (ungraded)

NP	Njovu Safaris	
	as above	

Renovated. Basic camping facilities and furnished rondavels with helpful staff.

Hippo Camp

NP	Lubungu Wildlife	Tel: (01) 22-9222
	Safaris	
	Box 30796	
	Lusaka	

A luxury tented camp, each tent with private ablution facilities. Walking safaris and boat cruises.

Kafwala Camp

NP	Busanga Trails	r8
	Box 37538	b8
	Lusaka	

Basic, self-catering camp.

Lufupa Camp

NP	Busanga Trails	r14
	Box 37539	b28
	Lusaka	

Well-known, established camp with furnished bungalows and camping facilities. Game drives and boat cruises.

Lunga Cabins

GMA	African Experience	Tel: (2711) 462-	r6
	Ltd	2554	b12
	Box 493	Fax: (2711) 462-	
	North Riding 2162	2613	
	South Africa		

Moshi Camp (derelict)
Musungwa Lodge
GMA   Box 92   r24
                Itezhi-Tezhi   b72
Well-established lodge overlooking the Itezhi-Tezhi Dam. Game drives, boat cruises, etc.

New Kalala Camp
GMA   Box 231   status unknown
                Itezhi-Tezhi

Nanzhila Camp (derelict)
Ngoma Lodge (being rebuilt)
NP   c/o ZNTB
                Box 30017
                Lusaka
Ntemwa Camp
NP   Box 37538
                Lusaka
Puku Pan (still under construction)

Lochinvar National Park

Lochinvar Lodge "D"
NP   c/o NHDC   r10
                Box 33200   b20
                Lusaka
Beautiful old farmhouse now grubby and mismanaged, has spectacular potential. Consult travel agents about its possible upgrading.

Campsite and chalets
NPWS
Secluded, leafy campsite. Basic ablution facilities. Helpful attendants.

Lower Zambezi National Park

Royal Zambezi Lodge
                Box 31455   Tel: 22-3952   b12
                Lusaka   Fax: 22-3504
Sophisticated tented camp offering walking, boating and canoeing safaris.

South Luangwa National Park

Big Lagoon camp
NP   being rebuilt

Chibembe Lodge "B"
GMA	Wilderness Trails	r6
	Box 35038	b12
	Lusaka	

Old-style luxury, game drives, walking safaris.

Chichele Lodge "B"
NP	c/o NHDC	r18
	Box 33200	b32
	Lusaka	

Somewhat mismanaged.

Chinzombo Lodge "B"
GMA	Chinzombo Safaris	Tel: (1) 211644	r9
	Box 85	Fax: (1) 226736	b18
	Mfuwe		

Luxury thatched bungalows.

Flat Dogs Campsite
GMA	Box 100	Tel: (062) 4-5074
	Mfuwe	Fax: (062) 4-5076

Camping facilities and self-catering chalets with shared facilities at reasonable rates. Game drives, night drives and walks.

Kakuli Camp
	Box 37783	r8
	Lusaka	b8

Kapamba Trails Camp
	Box 511843	r20
	Chipata	b25

Kapani Lodge
GMA	Box 100	Tel: (062) 45015	r6
	Mfuwe	Fax: (062) 45025	b16

Luxurious, old-style lodge; game drives and walking safaris.

Lion Camp
NP	Box 8164
	Kapiri Mposhi

Being rebuilt.

Luambe Safari Camp
NP
Derelict.

Lukonde Camp		
GMA	Box 77	r6
	Mfuwe	b12

Mfuwe Lodge		
NP	NHDC	r24
	Box 69	b48
	Mfuwe	

Comfortable, formerly state-owned lodge.

Nkwali Camp		
GMA	R Pope Safaris	r6
	Box 35038	b12
	Lusaka	

Sophisticated and luxurious bush camp.

Nsefu Camp "C"		
GMA	Wilderness Trails	r6
	Box 35038	b12
	Lusaka	

Old-fashioned but very comfortable thatch rondavels.

Savannah Trails		
	Box 30983	r6
	Lusaka	b12

Tena Tena Camp "E"		
GMA	R Pope Safaris	r6
	Box 320151	b12
	Lusaka	

An example of the ridiculous standards for grading, this is a very luxurious tented camp.

Tundwe Camp		
GMA	Sobek Adventures	r6
	Box 30263	b12
	Lusaka	

Simple reeded and thatched, furnished chalets with shared ablutions. Fairly reasonably priced, especially if you do your own catering.

Kasanka National Park

Wasa Lodge
NP	Kasanka Wildlife	r6
	Conservation	b12
	Box 32104	
	Lusaka	

Simple, reasonably priced, self-catering camp with clean, basic rodavels and shared facilities. Catering by prior arrangement.

Luwombwa Fishing Camp
NP	as above	r5
		b10

Simple, self-catering bush camp as above.

Musande Camp
	as above	tents

Kankonto Camp
	as above	campsite

Nyika National Park

Zambian Rest House
NP	R Pope Safaris	r4
	Box 320154	b8
	Lusaka	

Lovely, very old-fashioned self-catering lodge.

Sumbu National Park

Kasaba Bay Lodge "A"
NP	Circuit Safaris	r16
	Box 22890	b32
	Kitwe	

Effectively also run by a former parastatal, this lodge is not terribly attractive but has most luxuries. Also boats and game drives.

Nkamba Bay Lodge "B"
NP	as above	r16
		b32

More attractive but less organised than the above.

Ndole Bay Lodge "C"
    as above   r16
               b32
Pleasant and attractive.

Bangweulu game management area

Chikuni WWF Wetlands project
GMA   P/Bag 36   r5
     Mpika   b10
Self-catering camp.

Safariland Ltd
GMA   Box 36657
     Lusaka

OTHER LODGES/CAMPS/CAMPING FACILITIES

The following are tourist facilities not associated with national parks.

Fringilla Farm
    G Woodley Tel: (01) 61-1228 r7
    Box 31440   b20
    Lusaka
50 km north of Lusaka on the GNR. Very pleasant chalets, good restaurant and clean campsite with good ablution facilities. Riding, fishing and hunting on local farms arranged.

Hillwood Farm
    P and L Fisher
    Box 50
    Ikalenge
Proposed campsite as well as possible lodging as personal guests in a delightful farmhouse on a beautiful farm and game farm. On the road from Mwinilunga, beyond the source of the Zambezi.

Shiwa Ngandu/Kapishya Hot Springs
    Shiwa Safaris Tel/Fax: (01) 22-
    Box 36655   4261
    Lusaka
See chapter 10 for full description.

Tiger Fishing Tours Ltd

   A and B Esterhuyse Tel/Fax: (01) 26-
   Box 31730   2810
   Lusaka

Tiger-fishing camp on the banks of the Zambezi between Mongu and Lukulu in Barotseland.

Wildlives Game Farm

   A J Middleton
   Box 620089
   Kalomo

Camping facilities on a game farm not far off the Livingstone-Lusaka road.

13 MISCELLANEOUS INFORMATION

DRIVING TIPS AND SPARES

Because this book is principally aimed at visitors touring the country in their own vehicles it is as well to include some advice on appropriate vehicles, what spares to take and some general tips on driving conditions travellers are likely to encounter in Zambia.

As mentioned elsewhere, a four-wheel-drive is not absolutely essential to visit Zambia, but it would significantly extend the range of your travels. In principle, normal sedan cars would be limited to the main tar and hard gravel roads. The main camps in the Kafue, South Luangwa, Kasanka and Lochinvar national parks would be accessible, but more remote camps and national parks would not. There are not many places that a robust vehicle with reasonably high clearance such as a light pick-up or bakkie could not reach in the dry season. The smaller roads in western Zambia, which tend to be very sandy, are possibly the only routes not advised for such a car. The best option then is a four-wheel-drive and the best makes are strong, simple and popular vehicles for which spare parts and bush mechanics will not be a problem. Any number of different imported vehicle makes are to be found in Zambia. Government officials and those with the money drive spanking new Toyotas, although there are vast numbers of ancient and heavily abused old Land Rovers still grinding down Zambian roads under colossal loads. Bear in mind that armed car thieves and hijackers of Lusaka and the northern Copperbelt have a preference for new, white or otherwise anonymous looking pick-ups and four-wheel-drives.

Generally fuel is readily available with diesel and petrol equally in supply. Occasionally whole regions suffer brief shortages, so it is advisable to make regular enquiries. Fuel costs have been rocketing, but at the moment they are about the same as those elsewhere in southern Africa. Travellers should have a fuel capacity of over 100 litres and are well advised to always have one or two jerry cans of spare petrol over and above projected requirements.

It goes without saying that vehicles should be serviced before your trip – preferably weeks before so that ongoing problems can be ironed out. This is especially important in older model Land Rovers in which badly leaking oil seals can prove very irritating. Pack a comprehensive set of tools and spare parts. With regard to tools, a strong wheel spanner and good tyre levers, a puncture repair kit, a set of sockets and spanners ("imperial" for old Land Rovers), several screwdrivers, a tow rope, a strong jack and something broad and firm to stabilise it on soft ground may be considered essential. In addition, take jump leads, some electrical flex, insulation tape and a lubricating aerosol. If you are going into the bush take pliers, wire cutters and a role of stout wire. It is quite remarkable what you can make, fix or hold together with good wire. A hammer, hand drill and rivet gun, a wood saw and hacksaw, a shifting spanner and then a whole range of self-tapping screws and nuts and bolts may prove useful.

Spares: Definitely pack a litre or two of engine oil, gearbox oil and hydraulic fluid. A condenser and set of points, a spare sparkplug and a coil, coolant hoses, fanbelt and spare tyres and tubes may be considered essential. If doing an extensive trip a spare distributor cap and rotor are recommended. If the vehicle has an old-style alternator with detachable rectifier, regulator and brushes, take a spare set of these. Potholed roads wear down your undercarriage and a set of shackle bolts and bushes are a good idea (especially for old Land Rovers). Broken springs can usually wait to be replaced in major centres. Most of the listed parts can be found in the bigger towns, but they may prove expensive.

It is as well to have some mechanical knowledge and you certainly should not venture far from the beaten track in remote areas without it, but in most towns in Zambia you will find a bush mechanic to assist you. Ask at the fuel stations if there are any, otherwise at the Zesco offices. But be careful: many such mechanics have an intimate knowledge of car engines, but are not above using your misfortune to line their pockets. Negotiate prices beforehand. They will be extremely reluctant to do this, but you should insist on an hourly rate and knowing the price of parts. It is also advisable to accompany the "mechanic" when he goes off to fetch a spare part so that you can buy it from its supplier directly.

If despite all your precautions your vehicle still grinds to a halt, don't panic. More often than not the reason will be a simple one. If the reason is not apparent go through the possibilities systematically. Do not overlook the obvious.

First decide whether the fault is electrical or mechanical.

Mechanical faults are indicated if the starter motor turns over and there is a spark at the sparkplug leads but the engine won't take. Electrical problems can be more puzzling. Remember that in the electrical system components are connected to the positive terminal of the battery by leads and earthed to the body of the car, as is the negative terminal, thereby completing the circuit. If lights, hooter, etc., are not working, check the major earth leads connecting the battery to the body and the engine or gearbox to the body. If you have been doing a lot of bush driving it is quite likely they may have become disconnected. But if the lights work and the battery remains charged then test systematically back from the sparkplugs to the distributor, coil, solenoid, etc. A spare headlamp makes a good circuit tester.

The art of four-wheel driving is simply based on common sense and being gentle with your vehicle. If you have free-wheeling hubs, lock them before going into bad conditions. When it looks as if you are going to get stuck do not try and turn out of your tracks. Change down and try to proceed slowly. If you do stop, try reverse. Don't over-rev the engine and, especially in old Land Rovers, do not do that and suddenly release the clutch. That is how you break side-shafts. Try reversing, then going forward repeatedly a few times to clear a little running space. Don't push the vehicle to its limits – you will break something. Rather opt for the spades-and-branches routine. When driving off-road be very careful of tree stumps and holes. Go slowly through water and walk through it first to test depth (unless you are in areas where there are crocodiles!). If planning to ford deep water, make sure that the drainage hole at the bottom of the bell housing is plugged and unplug it afterwards.

Many African travellers these days pack hi-lift, jumbo or, as they are referred to in Zambia, Tanganyika jacks. They are extremely useful but also need common sense. If they are not properly greased they will not work. When packing do not secure them to your vehicle where they will get covered with dust and mud. If you do have to transport them on the outside of the vehicle, wrap the working parts tightly to protect them.

Check that they can actually be used on your vehicle beforehand. Some modern four-wheel-drive sedans simply have too many fancy fenders and so on to find a purchase. It is even possible to use such a jack as a winch!

DIRECTORY OF SAFARI COMPANIES AND TOUR OPERATORS

Acacia Safaris
Box 30475, Lusaka. Telephone: 27-2105. Fax: 27-4798.

Africa Bound
Box 31567, Lusaka. Telephone: 22-9154

African Experience Limited
Box 35944, Lusaka. Tel/Fax: 26-4256 or Johannesburg 462-2554
Fax: 462-2613

African Travel and Tours
Box 350036, Chilanga. Telephone: 21-5374

Andrews Travel and Safaris
Box 31993, Lusaka. Telephone: 22-3147/22-1582 Telex: ZA40104

Big Five Travel and Tours
Box 35317, Lusaka. Telephone: 221978/221098 Telex: ZA40091

Bonar Travel and Tours
Box 4211, Ndola. Telephone: 61-1185 Telex: ZA3410

Busanga Trails
Box 31322, Lusaka. Telephone: 22-1694 Telex: ZA40081

Busanga Travel and Tours
Box 37538, Lusaka. Telephone: 224761 Telex: ZA40081

Bushwackers Travel and Tours
Box 320172, Lusaka. Telephone: 25-3909 Fax: 25-0310

Chunga Safaris and Tours
C/o T G Travel, Lusaka. Telephone: 22-1867/22-6019

Circuit Safaris
Box 21491, Kitwe. Telephone: 21-2277/21-4447 Telex: ZA51750

Discover Business Tours and Travel
Box 86400, Lusaka. Telephone: 21-2302/25-3127

Eagle Travel, Tours Div.
Box 34530, Lusaka. Telephone: 22-9060/22-8605 Telex: ZA42670

Farland Tours and Travel
Telephone: 61-5060

Gwembe Safaris
Box 630067, Choma. Telephone: 2-0021/20-0169

Hunters Limited Africa
Box 33050, Lusaka. Telephone: 23-0576/28-7748 Telex: ZA40009

Iain MacDonald Safaris
Box 30684, Lusaka. Telephone: 22-8184/5 Telex: ZA40187

Island Safaris
Box 35943, Lusaka. Telephone: 21-4964 Telex: ZA45940

Jadason Tours and Safaris
Box 31212, Lusaka. Telephone: 21-1615 Telex: ZA45380

Jungle Safaris
Box 30050, Lusaka. Telephone: 28-7748/28-6706 Telex: ZA40009

Kafue Boat Tours
Box 30813, Lusaka. Telephone: 25-0772 Telex: ZA41390

Kafue Marina
Box 30743, Lusaka. Telephone: 21-4926/21-8964 Telex: ZA42830

Kazuma Safaris
Box 30793, Lusaka. Telephone: 21-3983 Telex: ZA40233

Lake Tanganyika Safaris
Box 20104, Kitwe. Telephone: 21-4905

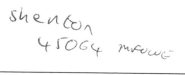

Luangwa Crocodiles Safaris
Box 37541, Mfuwe. Telephone: 21-4672/21-7023 Telex: ZA40129

Lubi Travel and Tours
Box 37782, Lusaka. Telephone: 22-3964/22-3216

Lubungu Wildlife
Box 31701, Kafue N.Park Telephone: 22-5650/22-3216

Lubungu Wildlife Safaris
Box 21701, Lusaka. Telephone: 25-3848 Telex: ZA41530

Magic Carpet Travel and Tours
Telephone: 22-2534

Mahogany Tours and Car Hire
Box 81349, Lusaka. Telephone: 25-1268

Makora Quest (Canoeing Safaris)
Box 60420, Livingstone. Telephone: 32-1675 Telex: ZA24018

Mercury Tours and Travel Agency
Box 32674, Lusaka. Telephone: 22-8975 Telex: ZA40217

Mulobezi Safaris
Lusaka Telephone: 28-8298/28-9056 Telex: ZA40292

Musungwa Safaris, Kafue N. Park
Box 92, Itezhi-Tezhi Telephone: 6-3035

Musungwa Safaris
Box 20104, Kitwe. Telephone: 21-5188 Telex: ZA51390

National Hotels Development Corporation
Box 33200, Lusaka. Telephone: 24-9144/8, Fax: 24-8352 Telex: ZA44140

Norman Carr Safaris
Box 30475, Lusaka/Mfuwe Telephone: 4-5015 Telex: ZA63008

Owani Safaris
Box 77, Mfuwe. Telephone: (062) 4-5017

Premier Travel and Tours
Box 37012, Lusaka. Telephone: 22-2931/22-4138/22-3324

Robin Pope Safaris
Box 320154, Lusaka. Fax: (260) 624-5076 Telex: ZA63007
Box 80, Mfuwe. Fax: (260) 126-0106 Telex: ZA42510

Royal Travel and Tours
Box 71853, Ndola. Telephone: 613-6261/61-4838 Telex: ZA33320

Safariland Limited
Box 33830, Bangweulu. Telephone: 2-1644/21-3404

Safari Par Excellence
Telephone: 28-7748

Savannah Trails
Box 37783, Lusaka. Telephone: 22-4457/22-4427 Telex: ZA40257
Fax: 22-4427

Shiwa Safaris
Box 1, Shiwa Ngandu.
Box 1, Chisamba.

Sobek Zambezi Expeditions
Box 60957, Livingstone. Telephone: 32-1432 Telex: ZA24018

South End Travel Agency
Box 60225, Lusaka. Telephone: 32-0773 Telex: ZA24027

Stamul Travel and Tours
Box 31541, Lusaka. Telephone: 22-1653 Telex: ZA40510

Summit Safaris
Lunga Luswishi Telephone: 21-6689/21-6318

Sunrise Travel and Tours
Box 34608, Lusaka. Telephone: 21-5903

Syndicate Safaris Ltd
Box 32904, Lusaka. Telephone: 21-6049

T.G. Travel Ltd
Box 32591, Lusaka. Telephone: 22-7807/22-6019

Ticcotravell and Tours
Box 410707, Kasama. Telephone: 22-1533

Tongabezi Safaris Ltd
Box 30832, Livingstone. Telephone: 32-0769 Telex: ZA24011
  Lusaka: Fax: 21-0400 Telephone: 21-6504 Telex: ZA40238

Top Flight Travel and Tours
Telephone: 22-4415 Fax: 22-4436

Transcat Tours (overland camping adventures)
Box 32540, Lusaka. Telephone: 26-1683 Fax: 26-2438

Voyagers Zambia Ltd
Ndola. Telephone: 64-0656/64-0241/2 Telex: ZA30078

Wilderness Trails
Box 30970, Lusaka. Telephone: 22-0112/5 Telex: ZA40143
Fax: 22-0116

Zambelina Safaris
Box 36147, Lusaka. Telephone: 22-9444 Telex: ZA40143

Zamtravel Tours
Box 30056, Lusaka. Telephone: 22-8681 Fax: 22-1205 Telex: ZA45121

CAR HIRE COMPANIES

Avis
Box 35317, Lusaka 10101
Lusaka Airport: Telephone: 27-1058
Fax: 27-1262
Headquarters: Cusa House, Cairo Road: Box 35317 Lusaka
Telephone: 27-2934 Fax: 22-1978

Car Hire of Zambia Ltd
Box 30083, Lusaka. Telephone: 22-2454

Omar's Car Hire
Box 30083, Lusaka. Telephone: 22-2454/22-1240

Ridgeway Car Hire
Box 30929, Lusaka. Telephone: 22-5209

Zamkar Car Hire Ltd
Box 23420, Kitwe. Telephone: 21-2884/21-1128

Zungulila Zambia
Box 31475, Lusaka. Telephone 22-7730 Fax: 22-7729 Telex: ZA40172

AIR CHARTER COMPANIES

Anderson Air Charter
Box 22671, Lusaka
Telephone: 28-6851
Telex: 43880

Bushveld Helicopters
Lusaka Airport
Box 35058
Telephone: 278357

Eastern Safaris Air Charter Lusaka
Telephone: 28-7508/23-3676/7
Fax: 23-3675
Telex: ZA40074

Government Communications Flight
Box 310291, Lusaka
Telephone: 27-1374
Fax: 27-1423

Lodge Hopper Tours Helicopter Travel
Box 2801
Nelspruit 1200
South Africa
Telephone: (27 1311) 58-1103
Fax: (27 1311) 58-1440

Roan Air
Lusaka Airport
Box 310277
Telephone: 271066

DIRECTORY OF FOREIGN DIPLOMATIC MISSIONS AND EMBASSIES

Algerian Embassy
Plot 42, Mulungushi Village
Kalundi
Box 33605
Lusaka
Telephone: 24-5945
Tlx: ZA40252

Angolan Embassy
Plot 6660, Mumana Road
Olympia Park Ext.
Box 31595
Lusaka
Telephone: 29-1142

Australia High Commission
Ulendo House
Box 35395
Lusaka
Telephone: 22-9371
Tlx: ZA44480

Austrian Embassy
30 A Mutende Road
Woodlands
Box 31094
Lusaka
Telephone: 26-0407/8
Tlx: ZA43790

Belgian Embassy
Anglo American Building
14 Independence Avenue
Box 31204
Lusaka
Telephone: 25-2344
Tlx: ZA40000

Botswana High Commission
2647 Haile Selassie Avenue
Box 31910
Lusaka
Telephone: 22-9371
Tlx: ZA41150

Brazilian Embassy
74 Independence Avenue
Box 34470
Lusaka
Telephone: 25-0400
Tlx: ZA40102

British High Commission
Independence Avenue
Box RW 50050
Lusaka
Telephone: 22-8955
Tlx: ZA41150

Bulgarian Embassy
Plot 251, Ngwee Road
Longacres
Box 32896
Lusaka
Telephone: 25-0880
Tlx: ZA40351

Canadian Embassy
Bank Buildings
North End, Cairo Road
Box 31313
Lusaka
Telephone: 22-8811
Tlx: ZA42480

Chinese Embassy
7430 Haile Selassie Avenue
Box 31975
Lusaka
Telephone: 26-2363
Tlx: ZA41360

Cuban Embassy
5574 Magoye Road
Box 33132
Lusaka
Telephone: 25-1380

Czech Republic
Plot 2278, Independence Avenue
Box 30059
Lusaka
Telephone: 22-1968
Tlx: ZA40272

Royal Danish Embassy
352 Independence Avenue
Box 50299
Lusaka
Telephone: 24-1634
Tlx: ZA40272

Egyptian Embassy
Plot 5206, United Nations Avenue
Longacres
Box 32428
Lusaka
Telephone: 25-0229
Tlx: ZA40021

Finnish Embassy
74 Independence Avenue
Box 50819
Lusaka
Telephone: 21-2739
Tlx: ZA43460

French Embassy
Anglo American Building
74 Independence Avenue
Box 30062
Lusaka
Telephone: 22-8030
Tlx: ZA41430

German Embassy
Plot 5209
United Nations Avenue
Box 50120
Lusaka
Telephone: 21-7449
Tlx: ZA41410

Ghana High Commission
7344 Nangwenya Road
Box 30347
Lusaka
Telephone: 25-4685

Guyana High Commission
Design House
Box 34889
Lusaka
Telephone: 22-6579
Tlx: ZA42960

India High Commission
Anchor House, Cairo Road
Box 32111
Lusaka
Telephone: 22-8374
Tlx: ZA41420

Irish Embassy
6663 Katima Mulilo Road
Olympia Park Extension
Box 34923
Lusaka
Telephone: 29-0482/29-0650/29-0329
Tlx: ZA43110

Italian Embassy
Diplomatic Triangle
Box 31046
Lusaka
Telephone: 22-8934
Tlx: ZA43380

Japanese Embassy
Haile Selassie Avenue
Box 3128
Lusaka
Telephone: 21-4661
Tlx: ZA41470

Kenya High Commission
Haramba House
5207 United Nations Avenue
Box 50298
Telephone: 22-7938
Tlx: ZA42470

Korean Embassy
28 Joseph Mwila Road
Fairview
Box 34030
Telephone: 25-1163/25-0728

Malawi High Commission
Woodgate House
Cairo Road
Box 50425
Lusaka
Telephone: 22-3750
Tlx: ZA41280

Mozambique Embassy
Mulungushi Village
46 Kundalile Road
Box 34877
Lusaka
Telephone: 29-0411/29-0451
Tlx: ZA43460

Netherlands Embassy
Plot 5280, United Nations Avenue
Box 31905
Lusaka
Telephone: 26-4254
Tlx: ZA43460

Nigeria High Commission
Bible House
Freedom Way
Box 32598
Lusaka
Telephone: 22-9860
Tlx: ZA41280

Portuguese Embassy
Plot 23, Yotam Muleya Road
Box 33871
Lusaka
Telephone: 26-3146
Tlx: ZA40010

Romanian Embassy
2 Leopards Hill Road
Kabulonga
Box 31944
Lusaka
Telephone: 26-2239

Royal Saudi Arabian Embassy
5th Floor, Premium House
Box 34411
Lusaka
Telephone: 22-7829
Tlx: ZA45550

Somalian Embassy
Plot G3/377A
Kabulonga Road
Box 34051
Lusaka
Telephone: 26-2119
Tlx: ZA40270

Russian Embassy
Plot 6407, Diplomatic Triangle
Box 32355
Lusaka
Telephone: 25-2183
Tlx: ZA40314

Royal Swedish Embassy
Kulima Tower, Haile Selassie Avenue
Box 30788
Lusaka
Telephone: 22-5808
Tlx: ZA41820

Tanzania High Commission
Bjaama House, United Nations Avenue
Box 31219
Lusaka
Telephone: 22-7698
Tlx: ZA40118

Uganda High Commission
Kulima Tower, Haile Selassie Avenue
Box 33557
Lusaka
Telephone: 22-7916
Tlx: ZA40990

United States Embassy
Plot 6407, Diplomatic Triangle
Box 31617
Lusaka
Telephone: 21-4911
Tlx: ZA41970

Yugoslavia Embassy
Plot 5216, Diplomatic Triangle
Box 31180
Lusaka
Telephone: 25-0247

Zaïre Embassy
Plot 1124, Parirenyatwa Road
Box 31287
Lusaka
Tlx: ZA217273

Zimbabwe High Commission
4th Floor Memeco House
Box 33491
Lusaka
Telephone: 22-9382
Tlx: ZA45800

DIRECTORY OF ZAMBIAN EMBASSIES ABROAD

Australia
High Commission of the Republic of Zambia
Box 517
Canberra Rex Hotel
Canberra City Act 2601
Canberra

Botswana
High Commission of the Republic of Zambia
Zambia House
Queens Road
Gaborone

Canada
High Commision of the Republic of Zambia
130 Albert Street
STL
1610 Ottawa
Ontario K1P5G4

France
Embassy of the Republic of Zambia
76 Avenue o'Jena 75116
Paris

Germany
Embassy of the Republic of Zambia
Bad Godesburg
Mittelstrasse 39
5300 Bonn 2

India
High Commission of the Republic of Zambia
14 Jor Bagh
New Delhi 110003

Japan
Embassy of the Republic of Zambia
9-19 Ebisu 3-Chome
Shibuya-Ku
CPO Box 1738
Tokyo

Kenya
High Commission of the Republic of Zambia
City Hall Annex
Box 48741
Nairobi

Malawi
High Commission of the Republic of Zambia
Box 30138
Plot No. 40/2, Capital Hill
Lilongwe

Tanzania
High Commission of the Republic of Zambia
Box 2525
Plots 5 and 9
Ohio Street
Sokoine Street Junction
Dar es Salaam

USA
Embassy of the Republic of Zambia
2419 Massachusetts, N.W.
Washington DC 20008

Zimbabwe
Box 4688
Zambia House
Union Avenue
Harare

INDEX

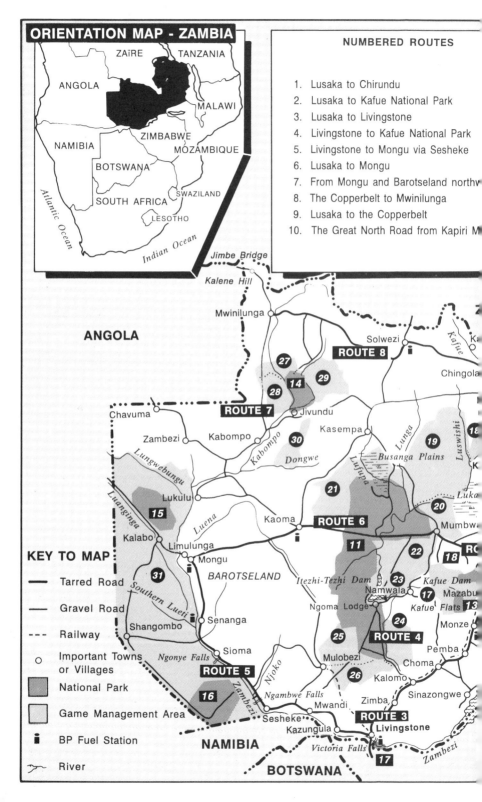

ORIENTATION MAP - ZAMBIA

ZAÏRE
TANZANIA
ANGOLA
MALAWI
NAMIBIA
ZIMBABWE
MOZAMBIQUE
BOTSWANA
SOUTH AFRICA
SWAZILAND
LESOTHO
Atlantic Ocean
Indian Ocean

NUMBERED ROUTES

1. Lusaka to Chirundu
2. Lusaka to Kafue National Park
3. Lusaka to Livingstone
4. Livingstone to Kafue National Park
5. Livingstone to Mongu via Sesheke
6. Lusaka to Mongu
7. From Mongu and Barotseland northw
8. The Copperbelt to Mwinilunga
9. Lusaka to the Copperbelt
10. The Great North Road from Kapiri M

Jimbe Bridge
Kalene Hill
Mwinilunga
ANGOLA
Solwezi
ROUTE 8
Chingola
Kafue
27
14
29
28
ROUTE 7
Jivundu
Chavuma
Kasempa
Lunga
19
Zambezi
Kabompo
Kabompo
30
Dongwe
Busanga Plains
Luswishi
Lungwebungu
Lufupa
Luanginga
Lukulu
21
Luena
Kaoma
ROUTE 6
Luka
15
20
Kalabo
Limulunga
Mumbw
Mongu
11
22
18
RC
31
BAROTSELAND
Itezhi-Tezhi Dam
23
Kafue Dam
Southern Lueti
Namwala
17
Mazabu
Senanga
Ngoma Lodge
Kafue
Flats
13
24
Monze
Shangombo
25
ROUTE 4
Sioma
Pemba
Ngonye Falls
Mulobezi
Choma
16
Zambezi
26
Kalomo
Sinazongwe
Njoko
Ngambwe Falls
Zimba
Mwandi
ROUTE 3
ROUTE 5
Sesheke
Livingstone
Kazungula
17
NAMIBIA
Victoria Falls
Zambezi
BOTSWANA

KEY TO MAP

— Tarred Road
— Gravel Road
--- Railway
o Important Towns or Villages
National Park
Game Management Area
BP Fuel Station
River